THE WORKING
LABRADOR

David Hudson

THE WORKING LABRADOR

SWAN·HILL
PRESS

Copyright © David Hudson 2001

First published in the UK in 2001
by Swan Hill Press, an imprint of Quiller Publishing Ltd

British Library Cataloguing-in-Publication Data
   A catalogue record for this book
   is available from the British Library

ISBN 1 84037 252 4

Typeset by Phoenix Typesetting, Ilkley, West Yorkshire
Printed in England by Biddles Ltd., Guildford and King's Lynn.

Swan Hill Press
an imprint of Quiller Publishing Ltd
Wykey House, Wykey, Shrewsbury, SY4 1AJ, England
E-mail: swanhill@airlifebooks.com
Website: www.swanhillbooks.com

Contents

Introduction

When colonels in their old tweed suits,
Are pottering gently round their shoots,
A Labrador's the dog they need,
Built for comfort, not for speed,
To plod sedately at their heel,
And dream about its evening meal.

David Hudson

To speak of 'working Labradors' smacks of tautology. I can think of no other breed that is used so extensively, nor for such a variety of work, as the Labrador. Labradors can be found working as guide dogs for the blind and hearing dogs for the deaf; as police dogs undertaking the full range of police work or specialising as sniffer dogs searching out drugs or explosives. They have been used to detect land mines, to search for bodies buried by snowdrifts, avalanches or earthquakes, and even to locate dry rot during property surveying. They are enormously popular as show dogs and are trained for obedience and agility competitions. Beyond that, thousands upon thousands of Labradors are kept as family pets and household companions, yet all this comes from a breed that was developed primarily for use as a gundog.

This versatility is carried over into the shooting field. As the name would suggest, the Labrador Retriever's original function was to collect dead and wounded game – a job that it will still do at least as well as and arguably better than any other breed. Excellent though it is at its prime function the modern Labrador is not limited to retrieving. It will work with the beaters in the woods to drive game over the waiting guns, or hunt and flush birds for the rough shooter on walked-up days. You will find Labradors hard at work among the heather of a grouse moor or the mud of the foreshore: in snipe bogs and flight ponds, at formal shoots where the bag is numbered in hundreds and on outside days where there may be nothing in the bag at all despite the best efforts of both dogs and guns.

The working Labrador may also be a family pet.

My intention in this book is to consider the working Labrador in its 'proper' role as a gundog while not losing sight of the other, and often equally important, role of family pet which so many working Labradors must also fill. Indeed, it is for the Labrador owner who wants to enjoy the company of his dog seven days a week as well as 'going to work' together on shooting days that the book is written. A working dog does not have to be confined to its kennel six days a week, and in the case of many a Labrador, its working days on the shoot may be occasional treats to be enjoyed away from its normal environment of house and garden.

So what is a working dog? Any dog that is taken to a shoot with the objective of being involved as something more than just a spectator is, in some respects, a working dog. A professional game-keeper whose dogs are at his side every day of his working life, perhaps beating or picking up four or five days a week during the shooting season, would almost certainly define 'working dog' rather differently from someone whose dog might do just a little light retrieving two or three times a year. In the same vein, someone who intends to enter their Labrador in retriever trials will have a very different definition of a 'trained, working dog' from the casual handler who takes the dog beating on a local rough shoot and may be content simply to turn it loose and let it go while trusting to its natural instincts to get the job done.

There are no strict divisions between the pet and the worker, the amateur and the professional. A field trial champion may also be a family pet, living in the house and playing with the children one day and competing at the highest level the next. Living with the family does not disqualify a dog from winning trials or working tests any more than living a Spartan existence in a kennel will automatically make it a better gundog. There are dogs that are kept solely as workers, housed in kennels and brought out only for exercise, training and shoot days, which show little, if any, signs of ever benefiting from even the most basic of training regimes. The fact that you only have one dog, and that it must double as children's pet, faithful companion, occasional watchdog and organic waste disposal unit as well as fulfilling its shooting role does not mean that it cannot be a top-class worker.

It may, however, make achieving top-class status a little more difficult.

Let us suppose that you are what we might term the 'average' working Labrador owner. You buy a puppy when it is eight weeks old, rear it, train it, and take it shooting for the first time somewhere between its first and second birthdays. Together you then enjoy eight, ten, perhaps a dozen years of shooting, whatever your particular type of shooting may be, before the time comes when you realise that this is going to be his or her last season. Stiff joints, failing eyesight and general debilitation mean that you must consider a replacement, and another eight-week-old puppy enters your house and heart. Given an average working span for both man and dog, you will probably repeat this scenario five or six times at most during your lifetime. In other words, you will train one dog at a time, separated by ten- or twelve-year intervals, and thus train a total of perhaps half a dozen dogs over sixty or so years.

Now consider the lot of the professional gundog trainer. You trained your pup in the evenings and at weekends when you could spare the time from work and from all the other commitments of a busy family man. For the professional, training gundogs *is* his work. You trained one pup this year and the next one twelve years later; the professional works with ten, fifteen, twenty or more new dogs every year. You had to compete with the rest of the family for the pup's attention and affection; the professionally trained pup will have lived in kennels and enjoyed a one-to-one relationship with its handler throughout the training period. All the good work that you were putting into the training may well have been cancelled out by the children playing games with the pup while you were at work.

The professional knows that his is the only influence on his pupils while they are in training – though it must be said the he has no control over what happens to them once they are returned to their owners as trained dogs.

You may never have trained a dog – never even have owned a dog – before starting out to educate your new puppy. Some people have an inborn knack, a natural talent, for getting a dog to obey them: others find getting such control over a dog is sheer hard work. You may be from either school, and it is only when you start training your first dog that you will discover which it is. And you may view training as simply a means to an end: something that has to be done in order to turn a playful puppy into a useful shooting companion, but hardly a hobby in itself.

The very fact that someone chooses to become a professional trainer of gundogs would strongly suggest that they started out with a keen interest in dog training plus a natural talent and considerable ability in that direction. 'Gundog trainer' is not an occupation that school leavers are guided towards, and as far as I am aware there are no colleges of further education offering gundog training as an alternative to sociology and media studies. Anyone training gundogs for a living does so because that is what they want to do; it is not the sort of profession that you can just drift into for lack of anything more interesting to do at the time.

In addition the professional trainer will have the right facilities: access to training ground and game when it is needed, a rabbit pen, perhaps jumping alleys and a pond for water work. Above all they will have experience, and will be continually adding to that experience. 'Practice makes perfect' is a cliché, but it is none the less true for that. We all learn from our mistakes, but when you only train one dog every twelve years or so you have an awfully long wait before you can put what you have learned while training one puppy into practice with the next. And assuming that, despite your errors, you finally turn out a dog that you can put to work on a shoot, you will have to live with the result of those mistakes for a long while.

But before you decide to abandon the idea altogether and leave the training to a professional, we might consider some of the advantages which accrue to the amateur trainer. Having only one dog to train means that you can give all your attention to that one dog. You can set your own timetable and take as long as you like – or better, as long as is necessary – between stages in the training programme. You will not have an impatient owner phoning you twice a fortnight to enquire when little Fido will graduate with honours. And since you are not being paid to train your pup you will not have to achieve a particular standard in order to justify your

Professional trainers and gamekeepers have advantages of experience, time and terrain over the amateur trainer.

fees. The only person you have to satisfy is yourself; you set your own standards, and you decide whether or not you finally manage to meet them.

You will only need to devote a short time each day to dog training. You can choose that time to fit in with the rest of your day. And if some days you are too busy, too tired, too ill or just not in the mood to go out and do some work with your pup then there is no imperative for you to do so. Your livelihood does not depend on producing a certain number of properly trained gundogs every year. You will not have another dozen pupils waiting for their lesson as soon as you finish with the first one. And you will not have to go out and work with your pup come rain, hail and snow, whether you (and it) like it or not. Being a Labrador it probably will not mind, but at least you have the choice. The professional has to get on with it, whatever the weather, or risk going out of business.

I mentioned standards. The fact that you are an amateur, training in your spare time and keeping your dog as a family pet, does not mean that you have to settle for an indifferent end product. Some of the best gundogs in the world have been family pets, trained by their owners. There is no reason why, given the right raw material, you should not produce a field trial champion (if field trials are your objective), or an absolutely superb shooting dog. It will all depend on the time and the care you spend on training, and also on the one limitation: the 'right raw material'. That is another major difference between someone who is training their own dog and the professional gundog trainer.

You buy your puppy, you bring it home and the whole family falls in love with it. By the time you begin training for work in the field, as opposed to the much earlier business of house training and generally civilising the little brute, it is so much a part of the family that you know that it is with you for the duration. What are you going to do if it turns out to have a hard mouth, an indifferent nose, a dislike for water or a general reluctance to shape up? Unless you are a rare exception, you are not going to cut your losses and start again with another dog. You are going to soldier on and make the best of what you have got. Unless its faults are truly awful the chances are that you will still have a lot of good times together. A hard-mouthed dog may not be an ideal retriever, but it can still be a great beating dog. If it hates the water it will obviously be a bit of a dead loss on the foreshore, but then you may not be a wildfowler. A lack of drive, or an excess of it, may be a problem but it will not be a problem of such magnitude that you cannot work the dog at all. It is a member of the family now, and what family could claim perfection for every member? And in ten or twelve years you will have the chance to start again with a new puppy.

The professional trainer of gundogs will – indeed, must – take a different attitude. If a puppy is truly hopeless, perhaps badly gun-shy, severely hard-mouthed, or just totally brainless, then it can be returned to its owner with a suitable explanation, hopefully before too much money has been invested in its education. There is a limit to the amount of time that a professional trainer will be willing to put into trying to educate an obviously hopeless case.

Others may be far from hopeless but have faults that mean they will only make moderate workers. For the trainer who is aiming for honours in competition, dogs that fail to train on to field-trial standard can be sold as shooting dogs. Those who lack any aptitude for the field may be offered relatively cheaply as family pets. For the worst cases there may be a bullet in the head and a hole in the ground. The professional will decide how much effort it is worth putting in to a particular dog. The amateur has just one dog to work with and whatever his ambitions that one dog will have to fulfil them.

When you watch a professional trainer handling a beautifully obedient dog at a shoot or a trial remember that you may well be seeing the best of a dozen or twenty dogs that have been through his hands in recent years. No gundog trainer can take every pup that comes his way and produce a potential field trial champion. All that he can do is to take the raw material on offer and shape it to the best of its potential. You can do exactly the same. The principal difference is that the professional deals regularly with a whole range of pupils from the brilliant to the dunce, from the timid to the headstrong, from those with tremendous potential to those who will never be anything more than adequate – at best. You will be working with just the one pup, and if fortune has not favoured you with the next Sandringham Sidney, then you are almost certainly going to elect to try and make the best of what you have been given. The professional can cut his losses at any time in the training process; you and Fido are together in this thing right to the bitter end.

The other side of this particular coin is, of course, that you may have purchased a puppy blessed with enormous potential and that the weak link in the chain may be you, not it. It is probably harder to get the best out of an exceptionally talented puppy than to turn a merely average pup into an acceptable worker. And of course, your definition of an acceptable worker may be different from mine.

There are owners who tear their hair out if their dogs make the slightest error in their work, and there are owners who blithely ignore the kind of behaviour that can all but ruin a day's shooting for their fellow guns. One handler may view the fact that his dog retrieved a cock pheasant that was lying dead in plain view when he had actually sent it to collect a second, wounded bird from across the hedge as an abject failure of discipline. Another may happily stand back and watch as his dog runs riot behind the guns, picking birds at random. There is no universal definition of what makes a good dog, only those standards that you set for yourself.

Good or bad, once it becomes part of the family the Labrador is there for the rest of its working life.

Hopefully, given the right breeding, your new puppy should have the potential to be turned into exactly the shooting companion you would wish for. A sensible approach to rearing and training your pup, particularly when introducing it to the shooting field, will mean that you should be able to turn out a gundog that meets your ideals of a good dog, and one that you can be properly proud of on shooting days.

I suspect that most of us would settle for that.

1

The Labrador

*The Labrador unquestionably holds premier position of all
breeds of working retrievers. – Lorna, Countess Howe*
'Hounds and Dogs'
The Lonsdale Library 1943

The Labrador retriever is certainly the most popular gundog
in Britain, probably the most popular in the world. Whatever
your involvement in shooting, from the formal, driven shoot
involving forty or fifty people to the loneliness of a wildfowler on
a salt marsh, the chances are that there will be Labradors working.
Even in the most specialised branches of the sport, such as shooting
grouse over bird dogs, there is a place for the Labrador, ambling
along at heel until the pointers have done their work, found birds
and produced them for the guns, and then taking over to retrieve
the shot game while the specialist game finders take a well-earned
breather. For the driven game shot, the wildfowler, the rough
shooter, the picker up and the beater, the Labrador is as much part of
the scene as the guns and the game itself. You might be forgiven for
assuming that there have been Labradors in the shooting field for as
long as there has been game to shoot, but in fact they are relative
newcomers to the sport.

Spaniels, pointers and setters have a history going back centuries
– back even before the beginning of shooting as a sport, when they
were used to flush game for falconers or to 'sett' birds in order
that the hunters might draw a net over the covey. The ubiquitous
Labrador, though, has been around only since the middle of
the nineteenth century, and was very much in a minority until the
beginning of the twentieth. The earliest reference to the Labrador in
my own modest library comes in *Stonehenge on the Dog*, first published in 1859. Surprisingly the section on the Labrador is not to be
found as might be expected in chapter IV, 'Domesticated Dogs
Finding Their Game by Scent, but Not Killing It, Being Chiefly Used
in Aid of the Gun', but in the following one, 'Pastoral Dogs and
Those Used for Draught', where it is classified alongside sheepdogs

In the days of muzzle-loading shotguns the Labrador was relatively uncommon.

and sled dogs. Indeed, the author refers to it as 'the St John's Newfoundland or Labrador dog', though the accompanying illustration by George Earl shows a dog that is built very much like the modern Labrador, apart from having a somewhat rougher coat.

'Stonehenge' writes:

> In Great Britain the small variety of the Newfoundland is seldom kept as a mere companion, being chiefly used as a retriever, either pure or more or less crossed with the setter or spaniel. He is then commonly known as 'a retriever' of the wavy-coated kind, to distinguish him from the curly-coated cross with the water-spaniel. Many of these retrievers are imported direct from Newfoundland to Hull and other ports trading with that island: others are bred in this country from imported parents, but most breeders prefer to cross them for the sake of improving the nose.

Fifty years later, in 1907, Mr G. T. Teasdale-Buckell was writing 'The Complete Shot', Methuen & Co Ltd:

> Recently there has been a great revival in numbers of the close and thick-coated, featherless dogs called Labrador retrievers. Their ancestors, or some of them, were, as the name implies, originally imported from Labrador. They were not Newfoundlands when first brought over any more than they are now. But it is rather difficult to say which sportsmen had one sort and which the other when both first began to be used for sporting purposes, or to be crossed with

setters and water spaniels, to make the ancestors of our present race of retrievers. The Labrador, as we know him now, probably had no setter or spaniel for ancestor, and there is every reason to believe that the Lord Malmesbury of the *Diary,* and later the Duke of Buccleuch and Sir R. Graham's family, maintained the breed in its original form. But probably in-breeding told the usual story: a cross had to be resorted to, because the dogs were getting soft, and one cross was introduced at Netherby, and of all the strains to select for a cross one would think that chosen the worst. It was a keeper's night-dog that was chosen.

The ancestors of the modern Labrador then are likely to be a mixture of the original dogs imported from Newfoundland, crossed with the working gundogs of the time and with a touch of mastiff thrown in here and there. The original dogs that were brought from Newfoundland were not gundogs at all, but were kept by fishermen because of their ability in water. It is said that they were trained to retrieve objects dropped overboard from the fishing boats and to swim from a boat to the shore when the surf was too rough or the coast too dangerous for the boat to land. The dogs would drag a line that was attached to a net so that men on shore could haul in the net and land the catch. The fishing boats would sometimes sail across to Britain to land their catches, and on occasion would sell a dog as well as the fish.

Their ability in water and their propensity for retrieving laid a solid foundation for a gundog: a foundation that was strengthened by crossing them with working gundogs to improve their noses and to import the gundog hunting instincts. The name 'Labrador' is believed to have been coined by the Earl of Malmesbury, who bought his first dog from a fishing boat that had landed its catch in Poole Harbour. He is reported to have said of the breed, 'We always call ours Labradors . . .', and the name stuck – otherwise we might be discussing 'small Newfoundlands'. At roughly the same time the foundations of other retrieving breeds were being laid, with our present Flatcoated and Golden retrievers being among the end results.

This surge of interest in retrieving dogs was primarily brought about by the development of the breech-loading shotgun, which in turn made possible what was then called the 'battue', or in modern terms the driven game shoot. Shooting before that time was a relatively leisurely affair, the pace of a shooting day being governed by the time it took to recharge a muzzle-loading gun once it had been fired. The sportsmen of the time certainly shot considerable amounts of game, but often only after long hours in the field and many miles of walking. The combination of the percussion cap and the self-contained cartridge, and thus of the breech-loading gun, made a new type of shooting possible.

Instead of the slow business of pouring powder and shot through the muzzles, then ramming down a wad on top of them and either charging the pan of your flintlock or attaching an explosive cap to the nipple of your percussion gun, you could simply operate a lever to open the gun, withdraw the fired cartridges and replace them, close the gun again, draw back the hammers and be ready for the next bird. Within a few years the cartridges would be ejected automatically and the hammers replaced by internal tumblers that were cocked as you opened the gun. Instead of taking perhaps a full minute to reload after firing a shot, by the late Victorian era a sportsman could recharge his weapon in the space of four or five seconds. If he was shooting with a pair of guns and a loader he could maintain virtually continuous fire for as long as the beaters could direct game over his peg. The age of the specialist retriever had arrived.

Before the days of driven game shooting a sporting gentleman setting out with his dogs and his gun would have to take himself to where the birds might be found. Whether he was intending to shoot grouse on the moors or partridge over autumn stubbles and turnip fields, the accepted method of shooting was to walk the ground. He might use pointers or setters to range widely and point game for him, or he might have a spaniel or two bustling just ahead of him and flushing birds within shotgun range. He might set out alone or with one companion, particularly when working pointing dogs, or might be one of a line of guns and beaters, wheeling and circling in a series of almost military manoeuvres that were designed to outwit the then common coveys of wild grey partridge.

There would (hopefully) be game to be retrieved, but the retrieving might well be carried out by the same dogs which were used to hunt and flush the birds. Even when specialist retrievers were used they would be required to walk with the guns, and the retrieving would be a sporadic task of a bird or two here and there as each covey was flushed. Generally the work would be 'hot' retrieving, the dog being sent to pick the birds almost as soon as each one had been shot.

Driven shooting, when it arrived, demanded an entirely different approach. At a driven shoot a dog was required that would sit beside its master, watching and waiting for twenty minutes, half an hour, perhaps even more than an hour, while birds flew overhead and were killed or missed in proportion to the master's ability. Then, at the end of the drive, there would be birds to pick – perhaps one or two, perhaps ten or a dozen, perhaps even hundreds at some of the more prolific shoots – and then it was off to the next peg to do it all over again.

You can train a pointer or setter to work as a retriever but it is first and foremost a hunting dog and it is never going to be happy sitting, waiting and watching while someone else has all the fun. The same is true to a lesser extent of spaniels. They can be trained as peg dogs, and some of them will work to a very high standard, but the heart of a Springer or a Cocker is in bashing through cover and flushing out game for the guns to shoot. The hunting dogs need drive and stamina and an eternal optimism to push them on to keep working when game is scarce. They are looking for the birds that *might* be there: when a retriever is sent to 'go fetch' it is usually after game that it *knows* is waiting to be picked. I say usually: we all know about those guns who have a bird down 'hard hit, probably stone dead . . .' three fields away, and almost certainly not a feather on it ruffled. My point is that a retriever ought to have a more patient and placid temperament than a bird dog or a spaniel: mostly they do.

Even the way they work is different. A good pointing dog should find its game on air scent (which is also called body scent): the smell of the actual bird as it crouches in cover. Retrieving may mean working on 'cold' scent: looking for game some time after it has been shot and, if the bird is a runner, following it up until it is found. A retriever must at times track a wounded bird using foot scent, hunting the invisible trail which the bird leaves as it runs, and ignoring the body scent of other game which it passes.

There is not a hard and fast division between game finders and retrievers, however. There are times when it is a great asset to have a pointing dog that can drop its head and track an old cock grouse as it twists and turns through a maze of peat hags, and of course, a great deal of shot game is found by retrievers using body scent borne on the breeze exactly as a pointer locates its birds.

The early development of retrievers was specifically to produce a dog that – as the name makes clear – would retrieve. There were pointing dogs and flushing dogs in plenty, but the new form of shooting had created a niche for a new speciality, and where there is a gap in the market there is certain to be someone who will find a way to fill it. Quite a few breeders tried, some with more success than others.

There must have been an enormous amount of experimenting, of mixing and matching the most suitable (and at times the most unsuitable) breeds of dogs before our ancestors arrived at the retrieving breeds that survive today. We have the Labrador, the Golden and the Flatcoated, all of which share similar ancestors, and the Curlycoated, which harks back to the old Water Spaniel breeds, and which, though something of a rarity in the shooting field today, was once the commonest of the retrievers. In more recent years the Chesapeake Bay and the Nova Scotia Duck Tolling Retrievers have supplemented the class in Britain, though neither are yet common sights on a British shooting day.

In a somewhat ironic twist the Labrador, which was specifically developed as a retrieving dog rather than as a finder of live game, is now regularly employed to do the work of a spaniel. But then, as we have already seen, plenty of spaniels do the work of retrievers.

So what is a Labrador? If you want a definitive answer I suppose you could consult the Kennel Club's official standard for the breed. This will tell you a great deal about the appearance of the dog but not much about its character, and it is the character that for me defines the breed. It is in any case a dangerous practice to generalise. While it is easy to describe a 'typical' Labrador, there is no guarantee that the pup that you have just bought, or are about to buy, is going to match the 'typical' specification.

Even so, we should have a look at what makes the Labrador such a popular choice, not only to do the job for which it was bred, but also for all the other tasks for which it has been trained over the years, and as what is often described as 'just a pet'. Bear in mind, though, that for every characteristic that I list as typical of the Labrador, there will be some that exhibit exactly the opposite tendency. Generally, though – and I must stress the qualification – *generally* your Labrador is going to come with roughly the following specification.

The breed comes in three colours: yellow, chocolate and black. Of these black is the most common, followed by yellow, with the chocolate variety coming a very poor third numerically. In passing, I was invited as a guest recently to a shoot where there were about half a dozen chocolate Labradors on parade – something of a surprise since I had never before seen more than one at a time out on a shooting day. I asked my host why there were so many. He spent a few minutes running through some fairly complicated family relationships, but the gist of it was that all were related, and went back to the same dog, which was owned by one of the guns. I made the obvious remark, that 'one does not often see that many chocolate Labs in one place.' My host thought for moment and then shook his head gloomily. 'No,' he said, 'and I've never yet seen one that was any good.'

In case you happen to be contemplating a chocolate Labrador please do not be put off by that particular sentiment. Most working

Labradors can be yellow or chocolate as well as the more common black . . .

. . . but black is by far the commonest colour.

Labradors are black, but I have no idea whether their dominance is because they have proved better workers than their lighter-coloured cousins or simply because black is a more common colour. I suspect the latter, and no doubt someone with a working knowledge of genetics, dominant and recessive genes and the like could explain it for you. I can give you one reason why a black dog may be a good choice, which is that when it goes charging off through the wood flushing pheasants in all directions, no one will be absolutely sure that it is your dog because there are likely to be plenty of other black Labradors present to share the blame. By the same token, though, when it makes that brilliant retrieve you may find others ready to share the credit. And of course, if you have trained it properly it is not going to charge off in the first place – hopefully.

Whatever its colour, the Labrador is generally described as a 'medium-sized' dog. This can cover a multitude of sins, from thin, whippety types to big, solid dogs which still show signs of that 'keeper's night-dog' cross which Mr Teasdale-Buckell so deplored when writing almost a hundred years ago. There is a tendency among some owners – usually those with the larger type of Labrador – to decry the smaller ones on the grounds that they do not have the strength to put in a hard day's work. But in case you are thinking that you must look for a pup which will grow into at least the canine equivalent of a welter-weight, I would remind you that a cocker spaniel will happily retrieve a hare – sometimes without requiring it to be shot first if it happens to be a bit slow off the mark. The ability to put in a full day's work is governed by the dog's determination and strength of character, not by its size or weight.

That said, a proper Labrador is noticeably more solid in build than a pointer or setter, though quite probably smaller in respect of both height and length. Where the setter is all leanness and light-ness the Labrador tends to strength, with a good spring of rib, a broad back, a solid neck and a powerful head. The coat is short and thick, with a dense undercoat to protect the dog from cold and wet. This is a dog that is expected to sit still beside a peg or out on the shore for long periods in the worst of weather, quite possibly swimming for a retrieve between times, and a warm, water-resistant coat is absolutely essential. Take a thin-coated pointer down to the shore, duck it in the tide a couple of times and then ask it to sit beside you in the frozen darkness for an hour or two and it will probably end up with a severe case of hypothermia. Even if it does not it is going to shiver so violently that the chattering of its teeth will probably scare away every duck within a 3-mile radius. A Labrador, given the same treatment will bear it all with every sign of enjoyment, especially if you can also provide it with a duck or two to retrieve.

And if there are no ducks, just sitting beside you is enough to keep most Labradors happy. Where setters and spaniels are always anxious to be up and doing, exploring the next bit of cover, the next length of hedgerow, or, in the case of most bird dogs, the next county, the Labrador will be happy to sit and think, or even just to sit. If you want to spend the whole day in a pigeon hide then a Labrador is the dog to take with you. The active sorts will sit and scan the skies for incoming pigeons; the more sedentary will probably curl up under your feet and sleep, at least until you fire the gun.

There are exceptions of course. There are Labradors that are almost as hyperactive as the liveliest of spaniels. I was standing with the rest of the guns at a break in the middle of a long, narrow wood one afternoon, waiting for the beating team to work their way through to us, at which point we would become the beaters and take the second half of the wood through to them. Within seconds of the beaters starting out, some 300 yards away, a young, black Labrador appeared at the ride, crossed it, and headed on to hunt out the second part of the wood. The odd pheasant departed stage left as it raced around, eventually returning to join its master just before the rest of the beaters and their dogs reached the standing guns. None of the beating team was particularly anxious to claim the errant hound as their own, and since there were at least half a dozen black Labradors in the line, any of which might have been the guilty party, not very much was said. To be fair, our team bore the sight of the flushed pheasants with a great deal of fortitude, possibly because we were going to beat that part of the wood, so any birds lost were lost to the team of which the dog and its owner were part. We might have reacted differently if we had been shooting on the next drive as well.

As it happens I knew whose dog it was, but he was not about to admit it and I saw no reason to point it out. The damage could have been much worse because the little brute was not really hunting out the cover properly. It was charging about having a good run in the countryside and any pheasants that it found were found by chance, not because it was actively searching for them. It was only a young dog and will probably learn to hunt properly eventually, though whether that will be a good or a bad thing is open to question. What is certain though is that it should never have been taken shooting in the first place since it was clearly nowhere near to being trained and ready. There are some Labradors which would have reacted in exactly the opposite way. Instead of racing off into the distance they would have stayed close by their owners, over-awed by the other dogs, the guns and the strange surroundings, which would at least have had the benefit of causing less disruption to the shoot. Even so, it is folly to take a young dog shooting before it is ready – of which more later.

That young dog had clearly not had sufficient training to be taken out on a shooting day. Indeed, I would question whether it had had any training at all. There is a school of thought among a few – fortunately a very few – gundog owners which holds that the best way to 'train' a dog for the shooting field is to turn it loose and hope it will copy the properly trained workers. In practice there is a far greater likelihood that the trained dogs will forget their lessons and join in with the new kid who is obviously having so much fun racketing about the place. This is not calculated to make the owner popular, particularly with someone who may have spent the last year or so patiently bringing on a young dog of his own only to see it led astray on its first outing.

The Labrador, however, is reckoned to be one of the easiest breeds to train. There is an eagerness to please its owner in most Labradors that is often absent altogether in some of the more lively varieties of gundog. Whenever I come into the house from any absence of more than a few minutes, Bess simply has to bring me something. It may be a glove, a hat, a sock, an old slipper or a lump of peat from beside the fire, but she just has to present her little gift and be praised for fetching it. Retrieving is what she does: pleasing the boss is what she likes to do best, and as far as she is concerned an old sock is exactly what I am needing as soon as I come through the door. In some ways it is. The old sock is not important, but the welcome is. And that is Labradors.

If we leave aside those Labradors that are engaged in serious professional duties such as guide dogs, drug sniffer dogs and the like, there are three main reasons why people keep them. Some are kept for their original purpose as working gundogs, some are primarily show dogs, and the rest – probably the majority – are family pets. And of course, there are no strict divisions between one kind and another, since a family pet may well be a show dog or a working gundog. I have to say that a successful show dog is unlikely to double as working gundog, but this is true of the majority of gundog breeds. With the exception of some of the hunt, point, retrieve breeds there is invariably a gulf between the working strains and those that feature in shows. This is unfortunate, but it is a fact of life. Breeders who incline towards showing will be breeding for looks: those who compete in field trials will be looking for working ability. And since we are on the subject, a few less scrupulous breeders will try to sell you a pup for whatever purpose you specify – 'show, work or pet . . .' – whether they have looks, working ability, both or neither.

At home in the water – three Labradors in hot pursuit of a wounded mallard.

There is no reason why your working Labrador should not live alongside the family in just the same way as it would if it were kept simply as the family pet. There are a few things that you will need to avoid, like allowing the pup to get involved in games of tug-of-war with the children, or encouraging it to chase rabbits, but if you are sensible the shoot day worker can be the family pet for the rest of the week.

It is the Labrador's temperament that makes it so versatile. They are typically devoted to their owners and anxious to avoid giving offence. A Labrador wants to please you, whereas certain other gundog breeds are much more concerned with pleasing themselves. If I am out in my garden on a sunny afternoon Bess, my Labrador, will spend the whole time basking in the sun somewhere within sight of where I am working. At the same time, Ghillie, a Pointer, will be racing around harassing the little birds in the hedges or looking for a gap in the fence so that she can slip off into the fields around the house.

Some gundogs, even when commonly kept as pets, are hard work. Pointers and setters are not really ideal unless you have lots of time and space to exercise them, and the same can be said of most spaniels. All that pent-up energy has to find an outlet such as

25

Putting a collar on your dog helps you, and everyone else, identify it.

chewing the furniture or escaping from the garden and taking off to find their own amusement. If you live near a busy road this may well prove fatal for the dog. Even if there are no immediate dangers from traffic any dog which is running loose in the countryside is a potential menace particularly where sheep, lambs, free-range poultry and game are concerned.

Naturally, Labradors are not immune from sheep worrying or from roaming wild in town or country, but as a breed they are less likely than most other gundogs to spend their days plotting ways of escaping from under your gaze. With their placid, friendly nature they are ideal with children and generally get along well with other dogs.

As with any breed of dog, their attitude to life is shaped by both instinct and training. If you allow your puppy to roam freely as a youngster you should not be surprised if it continues to wander when it grows up. If you allow it to adopt a dominant position within the family you will inevitably encounter difficulties when you try to make it do what you want rather than what it wants. The beauty of Labradors though is that they are generally less likely to suffer from social ills than almost any of the other gundogs.

But remember: I am generalising, and that is always a dangerous thing to do. Just as there are placid Irish Setters, and timid Dobermans, so there are Labradors that can be aggressive, dominant, hyperactive, anti-social and a generally bad advert for the breed. Fortunately they are far from typical, and choosing the right puppy, from the right parents will do a great deal to ensure that you don't get landed with one of the rare delinquents.

2

The New Puppy

Show, work or pet; they're whatever you need,
Dad's a show champion; Crufts Best of Breed,
And a beautiful nature: well temperament really is vital.
And Mother's from working lines, very well bred,
We don't shoot ourselves, but a friend of ours said,
That, if trained, she's a cert for a field trial champion title.

David Hudson

Choosing Your Puppy

If life were simple a Labrador would be a Labrador would be a Labrador and all that you would need to do in order to get your hands on the perfect gundog, show dog or family pet would be to find an advertisement in your local paper, phone the breeder and go along to make your choice. If only life were that simple.

Lots of breeders do advertise their puppies as suitable for showing and for work as well as for family pets, and it is possible that some of them may not be infringing the Trade Descriptions Act. Certainly, there is no over-riding reason why your new pup should not have the looks to win in the show ring and the temperament of the perfect pet coupled with the working ability of a field trial winner, and I have no doubt that there are Labradors around which have exactly that. I must add the rider though that you are extremely unlikely to find one in your local paper – or anywhere else for that matter.

It is unfortunate but true that the majority of gundog breeds are split between working dogs and show dogs. This is hardly surprising, given that the vast majority of the people who show gundogs do not work them, and similarly, the vast majority of those who work gundogs would never darken the doors of a dog show. Working a dog and showing one are very different, and in both cases can provide the participants with all the leisure activity that they will ever want. People do both show and work their dogs, but they are a minority. (In fact, most Labrador owners probably neither work nor show their dogs but simply keep them as pets.)

Because of this lack of overlap between show dogs and working dogs a split between the different types has occurred within the breed, as it has with nearly all the gundogs. A show dog is bred for its looks, generally with no real regard for its ability to perform as a gundog, a working dog for its ability, often with scant regard for its looks. Under these circumstances a divide is almost inevitable.

You might purchase a puppy with a long line of show champions on both sides of its pedigree and still end up with a first-class worker. Go back enough generations and both the show and the working strains will have common ancestors. You might buy your pup from a shooting man who has mated his bitch to a dog owned by one of the other guns in his syndicate, regardless of looks, and yet go on to win Best in Show at Crufts. And conceivably, the pup from the show winner might be a top-class working dog, and the one from the working dog could have the looks to sweep all before it in the show ring. These things are possible in theory, but I must warn you that they are unlikely in practice.

If you want a dog to train for the shooting field, then you should buy a puppy from a litter where both parents are proven working dogs. 'Proven' in this instance does not necessarily have to mean that the parents need be field trial winners, nor that there must be a scattering of 'FTCh' prefixes throughout the pedigree, though neither should you be prejudiced against the puppy if there is. It means that the parents should both be working regularly, should have soft mouths, good temperaments and the sort of build that you hope your puppy will develop eventually, and, ideally, should be dogs that you have seen working and admired for yourself.

If you know of just such a litter and you are in the market for a puppy my best suggestion would be to stop wasting your time reading this chapter and get along to pick the one you like. And of course, if you shoot, or work your dogs regularly on shoots, you are well placed to find out where there is a litter that might produce exactly the right puppy for you. Ask around and let it be known among the guns, beaters, pickers-up and keepers that you are looking for a dog and the odds are that someone will be able to point you in the right direction.

That was almost too easy, wasn't it? But what if you do not have the right contacts, or none of your friends knows of a suitable litter? Well, in the *Shooting Times* that I have just collected there are twenty-three advertisements offering gundogs for sale and thirteen of those are for Labradors. And all of them say the pups are from working parents. If you were set on a working Field Spaniel, Sussex Spaniel or Curlycoated Retriever then you might be in for a long

This handsome dog has been bred for its working ability, not just for its looks.

and difficult search before you could find any litters, never mind one bred from working parents, but with Labradors there is no such problem. Labradors are in a buyer's market.

So ask around, look in your local paper and the shooting press, and I can almost guarantee that you will find the right sort of puppy ready and waiting at an address somewhere near you. Now all you have to do is go and visit and if, after meeting the breeder, the dam and, if possible the sire, you still think this is a good choice, then you are ready to select the right one from the litter.

First a few words of warning. Neither your local paper nor the shooting press are able to check that every advertiser is telling the whole truth about his wares. When a seller says 'both parents working regularly', or 'from first-class working stock', or indeed that old mantra 'show, work or pet', they can do so in the certain knowledge that no one from the advertising department of the *Billingsgate Bugle* is going to be checking the truth of that claim before running the ad. At the risk of drifting into the realms of philosophy we might even ask ourselves the question 'What is truth?' – or, more specifically, what is truth as regards adverts for working Labrador puppies?

Beaters and keepers – likely sources of information on the whereabouts of good working puppies.

Consider the term 'working'. It could mean a keeper's dog that is used to dog in pheasant poults in the summer, picks up on the grouse moors through August and September and then beats or picks up on driven shoots three or four times a week from October through to the end of January. I think we can all agree that the title 'working dog' is fairly earned in such a case. But what about the family pet whose owners spend Christmas in the country every year and tag along with their hosts on a Boxing Day shoot to help make up the numbers and give the dog a bit of a run? The dog might actually do a useful job, rousting pheasants from cover or even retrieving behind the guns, but does that qualify it as a 'working' dog? The proud owners might consider the title well merited, but it is hardly a sound basis on which to assess the likely ability of its offspring.

Which does not mean that the once a year worker has not got the potential to be as good as the keeper's dog, nor indeed that the keeper's dog will automatically produce puppies that will grow up to become ideal workers. However, as the decision you are about to make is one that you will have to live with for perhaps the next fifteen years, your chances of getting a pup with the right potential are almost certainly better with the keeper's dog than with the occasional worker.

So when you go to see a new puppy, do not just look at the pups, or even just the pups and their parents. Unless you are buying

'Working' can mean many different things, from picking up on a grouse moor in August . . .

. . . to beating on a driven shoot in January.

from someone you know already, or who has been recommended by someone you trust, look at the owners as well. Consider where they live, what sort of lifestyle, what pictures they have on the walls, what sort of vehicle they drive, whether there are a few well-worn retrieving dummies hanging up with the dog leads, or muddy boots and Barbour jackets in the hall. Do they look and sound the sort of people who spend the shooting season out in the rain and the mud, working their dogs on a shoot? Chat about where they work their dogs, people you might know in common, what they think of the latest attempt by Parliament to ban/licence/regulate/proscribe shooting/hunting/fishing/guns or whatever. You should soon discover whether the pups really do come from the 'strong working lines' claimed in the paper. If you do not think that the pup's parents have the working experience that you desire, then thank the owners for their trouble and go and look elsewhere.

If the breeders really are dedicated to working dogs you are liable to find much the same sort of scrutiny directed at yourself. A responsible breeder wants to find the right sort of home just as keenly as you want to find the right sort of puppy. They should want to know where you live, what arrangements you have made to house the pup, whether there will be anyone at home during the day, what previous experience you have in rearing and training Labradors, and how and where the pup will be working. If all they seem to be interested in is foisting a pup onto you and collecting your cheque then think carefully before completing your purchase.

Ideally, if time and distance allow, go and see the puppies before they are ready to leave home – perhaps at four or five weeks old. This will give you a chance to see what sort of care is being taken of them as they are weaned: how clean their quarters are kept, how often and with what they are fed, and so on. It will also help you to make an initial assessment of the litter while leaving you a few weeks to think things over before making your final decision. Once they are eight weeks or older they will be ready to move to their new home and there will be a tendency for you to pick a pup and take it away with you there and then. It can sometimes be quite difficult to say no in the face of a persuasive seller and an appealing bundle of puppies, but it is much easier to remain un-committed if you can arrange a visit before they are ready to leave their mother.

Eventually the moment to make the big decision will arrive. You will have approved their breeding and their background and agreed a price: now all you have to do is select one puppy – the right puppy

Bold or shy: ideally your own temperament will match that of your chosen puppy.

– from among that wriggling, chewing, squirming bundle of bodies. How on earth do you do that?

The last puppy that I bought was a Cocker Spaniel, not a Labrador, but choosing her was easy – primarily because we did not. While Georgina and I were trying to pick 'our' puppy from the six or seven on offer one of them decided to pick us. She bustled to the front of the run and stood there saying 'Me, me, me' until our minds were made up. There was really no alternative, and 'Darcey Bustle' has been on the staff ever since. We have never regretted her choice: I trust that she would feel the same.

The first thing to decide is whether you want a dog or a bitch. Dogs tend to be a little more bone-headed and possibly slightly less easy to train than bitches but it is not a hard and fast rule. A dog is more likely to be aggressive than a bitch. A bitch will come into season a couple of times a year and you will not be able to work her for about three weeks each time which can be a nuisance if it happens during the busiest part of the shooting season. However, you can get your vet to give her a course of injections to prevent her coming into heat if it causes problems either with working her or with the unwanted attentions of the local dogs. There is an old cliché that says bitches are a nuisance twice a year, for three weeks at a time, whereas a dog is only a nuisance once a year, but it lasts for the full fifty-two weeks. This is a very sweeping generalisation and not necessarily correct, but there is a hint of truth about it. So: is it to be a dog or a bitch? There is no 'correct' answer, and you will have to make up your own mind.

Having settled the matter of sex (or not if you have no particular preference) the next thing is to sort out which pups you have to consider. If you are after a bitch, separate the ladies from the gentlemen, and vice versa. Then check whether any of the pups are already spoken for by other buyers or are being kept on by the breeder. This could cut your options down considerably. Once you have narrowed the field down to the definite starters you can begin to make a choice.

Take your time over this: you are going to live with the results of this decision for an awfully long while. Watch them playing among themselves and see which are dominant and which allow themselves to be dominated. Does one of them in particular seem to have taken to you? Pick them up and hold them and see how they react to you. Do they nuzzle into your shoulder or do they wriggle and squirm and try and get away? Have a good look for weepy eyes, any signs of umbilical hernias, or undershot or overshot jaws. Ask whether the parents have been X-rayed for signs of hip dysplasia and if so, how well they scored.

Think about your own personality and experience of training dogs. Would you be better suited with a bold, dominant puppy that may be hard work to train but which could turn into a brave, hard-going worker, or would such a dog end up dominating you? Would one of the quieter, more retiring pups fit in with you better, or are you the sort who might make it timid and reluctant to work? All this is much easier when you have already owned and trained a few dogs, but if you are a first-time buyer you should still try and make a best guess at the type of pup that will suit you, your personality and your family circumstances. You would not want to take a shy, retiring puppy home to a houseful of boisterous children. It is not an easy choice, and there is always every chance that the shy puppy may become much bolder and more confident once it has settled into its new home. And of course, you may find that the new surroundings cause a dominant puppy to shrink into its shell. Even so, at four or five weeks old their behaviour is a useful guide, though by no means an infallible one, to how they will turn out as adults.

The right choice is important, but bear in mind that there are two factors which decide how the puppy will turn out: how it is bred, and how it is raised and trained. Breeding supplies the

Even if you only intend to work your dog occasionally you should still buy your pup from proper working parents.

potential, but the raising and training translate that potential into whatever the puppy becomes in later life. I have seen various estimates of the relative importance of the two factors; some assert that 'it is all down to breeding' and others maintain that a good dog is primarily the product of good training. If one puppy really stands out in your opinion, then take it. After all, whatever the individual traits they are displaying now, they all have the same mother and the same father, so the inherited potential should be the same for all of them. And if you are really lucky one of them might do as Darcey Bustle once did for us and save you any hassle by picking you.

Early Days – Introducing the Pup to Its New Home

So the great moment has arrived and you are the proud owner of one Labrador puppy. You are about to introduce it to its new home, you are absolutely delighted with your choice and you cannot wait to start making friends with it. Now is the moment to spare a thought for how *it* may be feeling.

All its short life so far has been spent among the warmth and companionship of its brothers and sisters and its mother. Now, suddenly, a complete stranger has taken it away from the nest, very possibly shut it up in a cardboard box and taken it for its first ever ride in a motor car, and here it is, frightened, lonely, quite likely having just been car sick and with nothing familiar to turn to for comfort. You can understand if it does not really feel in the mood to start playing games with the children right now, or if it just wants to go and hide in a corner.

Of course, it may do no such thing. Some pups have an amazing self-confidence and will take everything that life can throw at them with a shrug of the shoulders and a wag of the tail. Even so, it will certainly find its new surroundings strange and possibly intimidating, and it is up to you to help it to settle down and build up its confidence. Beyond that, this is the first and possibly best moment to start forming a bond with your puppy. Hold it, sit it on your lap, cuddle it and tell it what a big brave dog it is, give it some little titbits to eat if it is hungry, and let it sleep if sleep is what it seems to want. In short, make it feel that this is not such a bad place after all, and that you – especially you, if you are going to be the one who is going to train it and work it – are its new best pal in the whole world. The bonds established now can last for the rest of its life.

I mentioned letting it sleep. You will no doubt have addressed the question of where it will be sleeping well in advance of bringing it home. To begin with, is it going to live in the house or have you got some sort of kennel ready?

If you've bought an eight- or nine-week-old puppy the first thing to remember is that it will not be house trained, so if your house is entirely carpeted in the best Axminster I can foresee some problems in the next few weeks. New puppies and new carpets make poor companions. You can try to protect the carpet with lots of newspapers, but ideally the pup's part of the house should have a floor that will respond to a wipe from a mop. And do not forget that puppies growing new teeth need things to chew on. In the absence of something more suitable the skirting boards, the corners of the doors or legs of your chairs will suit them quite nicely.

Your puppy does not know the rules yet and it is going to take it a few weeks to learn them. In the meantime, the best thing you can do is to try and ensure that it does not cause too much havoc. Give it something to chew – a bone, some sort of doggy toy, a rawhide chew bar, or possibly all three. And, particularly in the first few weeks, if you are not around to keep an eye on what it is doing, try and make sure that it is not exposed to temptation.

One solution which has worked well for me in the past is to create a little haven which is the pup's own piece of territory within the house. The Cocker Spaniel, Darcey, was provided with a tea-chest laid on its side next to the kitchen range, containing her blanket, toys, bones, and anything else she happened to drag in there. The kitchen floor was made of slate tiles so any little accidents were easily mopped away, and at night, or if we were leaving her alone during the day, there was an arrangement of wire screens to make a sort of cage which allowed her a certain amount of freedom while keeping her from having the full run of the kitchen. She loved it, and quickly became quite house-proud. She would drag her blanket and all her toys out every morning for an airing, then drag them all in again and rearrange them to her satisfaction.

Such an arrangement has several things to commend it. Darcey was a winter puppy and having the tea chest next to the range kept her from getting chilled. It was dark inside and provided her with a den where she felt safe and secure. And once she was shut in behind the wire screens there was nothing for her to damage other than the tea chest itself.

If you are going to kennel the pup right from the start you must make sure that the kennel is dry and warm and secure. If you have close neighbours it may help if it is reasonably soundproof since the pup is likely to be lonely and unhappy for its first few nights away from its mother, brothers and sisters, and is probably going to advertise that fact as the top of its voice. And even at eight weeks a puppy can make quite a lot of noise.

Kennels

What you arrange for a kennel will depend on the space you have available and, to some extent, on the depth of your pockets. A kennel can be constructed in a convenient outbuilding if you have something suitable available, or you can purchase ready-made kennels and runs from a number of manufacturers. The most important thing about any kennel is that it should be secure: that there is no danger of your pup finding a gap under the door or gnawing a hole in the wire and taking off to explore the world.

It should ideally consist of warm, dry sleeping quarters and some sort of run where the pup can play and also relieve itself. Neither need be enormous: even an adult Labrador will curl up happily in a box about 2 ft (60 cm) square, and a run 10 ft × 6 ft (3 m × 2 m) will be big enough for the pup to get a little exercise and to sit out in the sun on a nice day. It is a great help in keeping things clean if you can hose the run down and also easily get into the sleeping quarters to change bedding and sweep out. Even if you are planning on keeping your puppy in the house a kennel and run can come in very handy for those times when you want it out of the way for a while.

Do not underestimate the ability of a puppy, or a young dog, to escape if it sets its mind to it. It can chew through or climb over wire netting, or dig under the fence, in a matter of seconds, and the puppy that has escaped once is liable to escape again. Life outside the kennel is obviously more interesting than inside – always supposing that the pup survives its moments of freedom and does not end up under the wheels of a truck – and escaping can become a habit that is very hard to break. The answer is to start it off right from the beginning with a really secure kennel and run.

Try and make the run out of something like chain-link fencing or weldmesh panels. Ordinary wire netting may look secure, and may well be so under most circumstances, but a determined dog can chew its way through it in seconds if it suddenly decides that it has a pressing reason to go over the wall. A bitch in season, or seeing you go off without it, may be all that it takes the first time, and once it has discovered that it can chew through the netting the run will never be safe again. At that point you will have to replace the wire netting with something more secure. It makes sense therefore to start off with one of the more expensive but hardy materials. The initial outlay may be higher but it will save you money eventually.

The sleeping quarters do not have to be palatial, but they should have a bed, raised off the floor away from cold draughts, and you should make sure that you can get at the inside for cleaning. A small sleeping box within the kennel can be ideal, particularly during the winter, when an outdoor kennel can become very cold at nights, but make sure that you can easily clear out the old bedding and sweep up straw dust and the like. Wheat straw (but not barley straw which can cause skin irritation) makes excellent bedding but needs changing regularly since it quickly breaks down and becomes dusty. Dogs love clean straw and will burrow in it and scrape it about with great enthusiasm until they have the bed arranged to their satisfaction. Old blankets, proprietary dog bedding materials such as Vetbed and polystyrene-filled beanbags are all suitable substitutes for straw, but all share the same disadvantage that they can easily be chewed up by a bored puppy.

The outside run, unless it is very large, is best floored with flagstones or concrete. A small grass run will quickly turn into a morass during wet weather as well as being very difficult to keep clean. Stone or concrete can be hosed down and treated with disinfectant, and will help to keep your pup's claws worn down. Make sure that there is a human-sized entrance to the run as well as a pop-hole from the kennel. I once had a kennel that was designed so that the only way to get into the run was to crawl through a hole about 2 ft (60 cm) square in the front of the sleeping quarters. It was fine for the dogs but not a pleasant experience for me, bearing in mind that the reason for crawling through that hole was to shovel up whatever had been deposited in the run. Ideally you would incorporate a drain and a soakaway pit into the design, but if you are siting your kennel on some existing hard standing this may not be practical.

House Training

One of the first things that you will have to do with the pup is to set about house training it. This is obviously essential if it is going to live indoors, and even if it is going to live in a kennel there may be times when you will want to bring it into the house. The sooner it learns the basic rules the better.

At eight weeks old a puppy functions pretty much by instinct. When it wants to go it is going to go and never mind that you paid £35 a metre for that piece of Axminster. It will serve it just as well as a strip of grass or an old newspaper. It does not know any better, and certainly does not do it with any malicious intent. So how are you going to survive the first few weeks until it becomes 'safe' in the house?

There are two keys to house training. One is that, much of the time, you can predict when your pup will need to go: whenever it wakes up, after a meal or a drink, after it has been playing for a while, first thing in the morning and when you come home after it has been left alone. The trick is to anticipate its needs and take it outside before it can perform in the house.

The second key is that puppies are creatures of habit. Your task is to ensure that yours develops good habits rather than bad ones. Thus you must get it into the habit of going into the garden whenever it needs to empty its bladder or bowels – into a particular part of the garden if you wish – and eventually it should get the message. You are bound to have a few accidents along the way, unless you are exceptionally lucky, and it is up to you keep the damage down to a minimum. The pup has no way of distinguishing between the kitchen lino and the drawing room carpet and would not care even if it could.

It may already be partly conditioned to look for a sheet of news-paper when it needs to relieve itself. Many breeders use old papers to line whelping boxes or spread them on the floor where the pups are playing. A paper on the floor close to the pup's bed, or inside its cage if you are using one, will make cleaning up the inevitable mistakes a lot easier. It will also condition the pup to using a sheet of newspaper in a particular place as its 'emergency' toilet for those occasions when you are too slow to pop it out into the garden, or when you are simply not around. Otherwise it will select a suitable spot using its own judgement, and since its criteria will be different from yours, the 'suitable spot' may turn out to be right in the middle of a Chinese silk rug. And once it has identified its suitable spot it will keep going back to it again and again.

House training may be easier if you are buying an older puppy. Note that I say '*may* be easier', it is by no means certain. An older dog should be quicker to understand what you want from it, and will certainly not need to relieve itself with the same frequency as a puppy. And if it has been reared in the breeder's home it should have had some house training already. That much is in your favour. On the other hand, if it has been living in a kennel it will not have been in the habit of waiting to be put outside before going, and when it does go there will be a lot more to shovel or to mop up.

Some pups are remarkably quick to understand what is required of them; others take longer. You just have to be patient and not invite the boss over for dinner for a week or two. There is no point in getting angry with a puppy simply because it has behaved according to its instincts, and in particular there is no use what-soever in smacking it, shaking it or rubbing his nose in the mess. Take it out into the garden every time you think it might be about to perform, and take it out anyway even if you do not. Praise it whenever it performs outside and before too long it will be asking to be let out when it feels the need.

Your aim is to establish in the pup's mind that the right and proper place to relieve itself is out in the yard and not in the house. As the habit becomes established it will quickly understand the routine. You should also develop the habit of popping it outside regularly, and making sure that it has relieved itself before it comes back in – particularly when the weather is cold and wet. The time taken to house train a puppy varies considerably between individuals, but it really should not take very long – it just some-times *feels* as if it is taking forever!

Feeding

There are any number of proprietary brands of puppy and dog food on the market, some suitable for each and every dog and others specially formulated for animals of particular ages and conditions of health. In addition there are lots of books and articles available on various aspects of canine nutrition – some excellent, some less so and some frankly full of crackpot notions. I would strongly recommend that to begin with you find out what the breeder has been feeding your pup and get some of that to feed it on for the first few days. The breeder may well offer to provide you with enough food for a day or two to start you off. The last thing you want is for the pup to begin life in its new home with an upset stomach brought on by a change of diet. It is the last thing your carpets need as well.

If you decide not to continue feeding it the same food as the breeder it would be best to make the change gradually over two or three days. And before you purchase several kilos or so of *your* favourite brand it is as well to try the pup out with a sample just in case *it* does not like it.

Fortunately, Labradors are rarely difficult to feed, generally being the canine equivalent of a waste disposal unit or an industrial sludge pump. There are plenty of hard working dogs that are fed mainly on table scraps, though the suitability of such a diet will depend largely on the type of table you set and the amount of scraps left over. I do not imagine that any dog would fare well if it was fed on the scraps from a family of dedicated vegans.

Proprietary brands of food, whether you feed tinned meat with biscuits or one of the 'complete' diets available to be fed either dry or mixed with water, vary in price from the reasonable to the horren-dously expensive. Do not imagine for one moment that 'dearer' necessarily means 'better' in the dog food market. Compare the contents, not the price. There are some dog owners who will happily pay a fortune for a bag of dog food in the mistaken belief that, because it is ridiculously expensive, they must therefore be getting the best possible food for little Fido. Not surprisingly, there are plenty of manufacturers who will happily hike up their prices to accommodate them. You should not fall into the same trap – unless you particularly want to, in which case spend away; it is your wallet, and it will not do the pup any harm. Nor, though, will it do it any particular good.

When you first bring it home at around eight weeks old the pup will need several small meals a day – say two milk-based feeds alternated with two solid ones. Check with the breeder to see what routine he was following and then adapt it gradually to suit you and your new pup. Beware of starting the pup off on a feeding routine that you will not be able to sustain. Half a kilo of steak mince mixed with biscuits will probably be enough for four or five feeds when the pup is eight weeks old, but it will swallow the whole lot in one mouthful a few months later, at which point feeding it on best butcher's meat will become very expensive, particularly if this diet makes it become faddy about its food and turn its nose up at normal rations.

Do not overfeed: a fat puppy may look bonny but the extra weight will put unnecessary strain on growing joints and some nasty – and expensive – ailments can result. A Labrador puppy should look neither fat nor excessively skinny. Some pups seem to burn up an awful lot of calories as nervous energy while other, more placid ones will put on weight rapidly if fed the same diet. A puppy may have odd spurts of growth that will leave it looking lean and leggy for a week or two, possibly mixed with other times when it doesn't seem to grow at all.

Gradually reduce the number of meals you feed the pup. By six months two meals a day should be sufficient and at a year old the dog should have been switched to its adult feeding regime. This can be designed to fit in with your particular lifestyle: dogs are very adaptable, provided that they know what to expect. One meal a day in either the morning or the evening or the same amount of food split into two servings will be fine, provided you stick to a routine and do not just offer food as and when you have a moment to spare.

Some owners feed once a day, some prefer to split the rations between a small meal in the morning and a larger one in the evening. There is a school of thought that says a dog will work better if it has some food in its stomach before starting the day, but there is another that says working too soon after a meal can cause potentially serious problems such as a twisted gut. It is never advisable to allow a dog to race about too soon after having a meal, but if you give a light meal first thing in the morning it should be sufficiently digested to cause no problems by the time you start work.

The manufacturers' instructions are no more than a guide to the quantity you should be feeding each day, influenced in some cases more by the desire to sell dog food than to keep the customers at their best fighting weight. In any case, dogs vary enormously in the efficiency with which they convert their food and a diet that would make one Labrador fat might leave another painfully thin. Use your own judgement, not forgetting that a dog that is working hard during the cold months of the year is going to need a lot more calories than one that is lazing about on the lawn during the summer.

You must ensure that there is plenty of clean, fresh water available at all times, particularly if you are feeding one of the dry, all-in-one foods. Never allow your puppy to chew cooked poultry or rabbit bones that may splinter, though a good, meaty beef bone will keep a pup happy for hours as well as providing exercise for teeth that might otherwise be working on your furniture. Little treats are always welcome and can be used as bribes during training. Beware of chocolate sold for human consumption which, though invariably popular with dogs, can cause serious illness if fed in any quantity. If you want to feed your pup chocolate treats make sure that you buy the kind that are made specifically for dogs.

Inoculations

At about twelve weeks old your puppy will need inoculating against a range of unpleasant canine diseases such as distemper, leptospirosis, parvo virus and the like. It may be worth checking with your veterinary surgery before you collect your puppy to see if they have any special recommendations because of any local outbreaks, otherwise you should present it for its first jab when it is twelve weeks old. There are two injections, usually given with a fortnight between them. You have to wait until the pup is twelve weeks so that the parental immunity has worn off sufficiently for the inoculation to be effective, and until it has had both jabs you should keep it away from strange dogs and from places such as public parks where it might pick up an infection. If you are buying an older puppy, it may have been inoculated already, in which case the breeder will supply you with the documents confirming what vaccine was given, when and by which vet. The dog will also require a booster shot at yearly intervals.

All puppies need worming regularly. Check with the breeder when they were last treated and then get your vet to advise you on when and with what to worm your puppy. Note that the fact that it shows no signs of worms does not mean that it does not need dosing.

Young dogs will often exercise themselves simply by playing in the garden.

Exercise

At eight weeks old your pup will pretty much exercise itself. Young pups spend a great deal of their time sleeping and at this stage sleep is more important to them than exercise. They will typically spend a few minutes playing or racing about and then crash out quite suddenly and sleep until they are ready to play again. Never allow the children to force a pup to play when it would rather be sleeping.

The best way to exercise a pup is to let it play in the garden (assuming that you have made sure that your garden is secure before bringing the puppy home). Let it explore, let it race around and chase its tail or carry its toys about the place, let it lie on the grass and chew its bone and, if it wants to sleep, let it sleep. What it does not need at this stage in its young life is to be put on a lead and dragged around the streets for miles every day.

Too much exercise can put unwanted strain on young bones and joints. Hips and shoulders are especially vulnerable and problems started now can plague a dog for the rest of its life. Short, gentle walks are fine and will help build confidence, but never overdo things. As the puppy gets older you can gradually increase its exercise, getting it used to being on a lead, to meeting other people and other dogs, to seeing traffic and farm stock and reacting accordingly. In other words you can begin its training.

3

Basic Training

. . . Perseverance in the breaker is necessary at all times, to insure the same quality in the pupil. 'Stonehenge'
'The Dog in Health and Disease'
Longmans Green and Co

Setting the Ground Rules

It is no longer done to refer to 'breaking' a dog: it is a term that has unacceptable connotations of harshness and cruelty. In fact, when 'Stonehenge' was writing back in 1859, it was used in much the same way that 'training' is employed today. 'Dog breaker' meant 'dog trainer' and not necessarily someone who whipped his unfortunate pupils into submission. There is no doubt that some trainers then were very hard on their dogs but it was by no means universal, nor did cruelty die out with the end of Victoria's reign. If you substitute 'trainer' for 'breaker' in the quote above then it is as applicable to training a dog today as it was in the nineteenth century.

In any case, you will not want to 'break' your puppy, but to build a partnership with it. The first thing to remember is that you will not be equal partners in the venture. One of you is going to be the senior partner, and if the partnership is to flourish in the way you would hope, that position must be occupied by you, not by the dog.

A dog is a pack animal. Once it settles into its new home its 'pack' will comprise you and the rest of your family, including any other dogs or cats that you have in residence. It is important that it is not allowed to assume that its position is pack leader. In its mind you must to be superior to it in the pecking order, if you are not you are fighting a losing battle from the beginning. And it is often right at the beginning that the pecking order becomes established. Taken from its original family and catapulted into a new home, it is only natural that your puppy will need to establish its own position within its new family. It has to know where it stands – you have to ensure that it is in the right position.

Some dogs are naturally more inclined to be dominant than

47

others. Your puppy may accept you as the boss right from the start and never challenge that assumption, but, particularly if it was the dominant one in the litter, it may see itself as pack leader from the moment it settles in. If so it needs to be disabused of that notion as quickly as possible. The third possibility, and probably the most common, is that it will settle in initially in a subservient position within your household hierarchy, but start to question your authority as its confidence grows. This may happen at some time during its training or it may be delayed until after it has started to work on the shoot. The important thing is to recognise the challenge and to react accordingly.

Consider the new puppy, just away from its parents for the first time. Suppose you have made it up a comfortable spot in a tea chest in the kitchen. It's had a last trip to the garden to relieve itself; you've tucked it up in its box with a bone to chew and a bowl of water, put out the lights and gone to bed. Then it starts to howl: it's lonely and would really like to come upstairs and sleep on the bed or at least in the bedroom with you. Are you going to go down and bring it up, 'just for the one night, so that you can get some sleep'? If so, it has won the first round and set a very bad precedent. It knows that it can get *you* to do what *it* wants. That is not a suitable basis for your future partnership. If you want it to sleep upstairs anyway then fine, but it has to be at your instigation, not the pup's. In the same vein, if you do not mind it climbing into the armchairs then let it. If you want it to stay off the furniture then provide it with an alternative – a comfortable basket, a beanbag, or that tea chest – and gently but firmly insist that it uses it.

You must be consistent. It is no good letting your pup sleep in the armchair one day and ordering it off it on another. All you will do is confuse it, and dogs need to understand life in simple terms: black and white, right and wrong. Learning the rules is hard enough for a pup without it being allowed to do a thing one day and then being told off for the same thing the next.

Suppose that you have decided that whenever you let the pup out into the garden you will first make it pause on the doorstep until you tell it to 'get on'. You can do this from day one, even when you carry it to the door to pop it out for a comfort break. Open the door, set it down on the step, hold it for a second or so and then say 'get on' and let it run outside. As it gets bigger and runs to the door itself, hold it back – telling it to 'sit' first if you have progressed to that stage – and then tell it to 'get on'. It is going to take no more than a couple of seconds each time you let the pup out, but it estab-lishes two valuable lessons. First you will be reinforcing your senior partner position. The dog wants to race off into the garden, but does not get to do it until you give permission. Secondly, you are giving it its first example of good manners: teaching it that it is not its right to go rushing through the door ahead of everyone else. This sets a useful precedent for when it starts travelling and you do not want it to leap out of the car as soon as the door is opened, or at the shoot so that it does not go charging off into a covert as soon as the gate is pulled aside.

You can do the same thing when you feed your pup. When you bring its bowl of food, do not let it just rush up and dive into it. Hold the food up so that the pup is looking up and gently push its backside down into a sitting position, saying 'sit' as you do it. Then put the bowl down and hold the pup just for a couple of seconds before saying 'get on' and letting it at the food. Again, you are establishing that the dog does something it wants when you say so, not just when the impulse strikes it. As it learns what is required you can extend the pause a little bit and get it to stay without any physical restraint.

The most important part of this, though, is that you *must be consistent.* It is no use letting the pup charge through the door one day and telling it off for doing the same thing the next, nor making it pause before eating one meal while allowing it to tear into the next one unrestricted. And you must ensure that the rest of the family know the rules and keep to them as well.

Starting Training

In a sense you start training your pup from the moment you get it. At eight weeks old every day is a new learning experience, and while you may be establishing a few ground rules as you go along there is nothing to be gained from starting 'proper' training too soon. Puppies need to be puppies; they need to romp and play and enjoy themselves while they are growing up. Even so, there are some lessons that will need to be instilled during those early months. To begin with your puppy is going to have to learn its own name, which is simply a matter of selecting a name and using it. It should preferably be simple and sensible and something not easily confused with a word of command. You might feel like naming it 'Twit' but it sounds too much like 'sit' and will cause problems later on.

It is going to have to get used to wearing a collar and lead. The first time you put a lead round its neck can be quite dramatic; some pups react like a hooked salmon, leaping and rearing all over the place. If your pup reacts like this, calm it down, make a fuss of it, and do not keep the lead on for too long. It may help if you let it trail

A lead is an essential item for the Labrador trainer.

it around for a few minutes, though you must make sure that it cannot get snagged and give the pup a worse fright. It should soon realise that the lead is not going to hurt it, and that wearing it may be a precursor to something pleasant, like going for a walk.

When you are out exercising in the garden, the park or the fields you should call the pup by name and make a fuss of it when it responds. If it ignores you, do not get angry, and do not get more and more frantic in your calls. If it has decided that digging a hole or chasing a butterfly is more important than answering its name then all repeated calling will do is to teach it that it *can* ignore the call if it wants to. Do not call it if you think it is unlikely to respond: walk, or better still run, up to where it is digging and pick it up or put the lead on.

If you cannot walk up to the pup and it is not listening, you may find that walking away will bring it scampering to you. Alternatively you can try hiding. As long as it can see you or hear you shouting its name, it knows where you are and that it can come back to you when it feels ready. If you disappear there is a good chance that a lot of the pup's confidence will disappear with you. Once it does come back make a fuss of it: do not punish it. If you tell it off it will assume it is in trouble for coming back, not for its earlier failure to respond – which it has long forgotten even if you have not.

Most Labrador Retrievers are only too keen to live up to the 'retriever' part of their name and your pup is likely to spend much of its young life fetching you things and carrying things around. Always praise it for bringing you something, even if it is something you would rather not have been presented with, and never snatch things away or play tug-of-war with it. And if you have a family make sure that the children do not do it either. Throw a toy or a ball for the pup to fetch by all means, but don't overdo it. It is better to stop just before the pup has had enough rather than just after. Life for a puppy should be fun; there is plenty of time to get serious about things later on when it is grown up.

There is no 'right' age to begin a more formal approach to training, though you are probably better to start later rather than earlier. Six months would be a minimum for most pups, and some would be better left several months longer. This does not mean that the pup should be allowed to run riot and do whatever it wants from the time you collect it until the day you 'start' training. In particular, taking it out into the woods to 'see how it reacts' to pheasants or rabbits is not a good idea at all, nor is allowing it to race around the countryside completely unchecked. Incidentally, never, ever allow your pup to roam about on its own without some form of supervision. A dog that develops a taste for wandering is likely to end up as a road casualty or a sheep worrier. If your garden is not secure then make it secure, or build an escape-proof run – preferably before the problem can begin.

The Basics

No matter what breed of gundog you are training, nor for what purpose, all training is based on similar foundations. The dog should sit or drop on command and must come back to the handler when it is called. Teach those two things properly and you are well on the way to training the dog. There will still be a lot of other things for you to teach it, and even more things that it must learn for itself, but once those two things are firmly ingrained the right foundations will have been laid for everything that follows. In the case of retrievers the need to walk at heel is also important, and can be taught at the same time as you are teaching the 'sit' command.

Your dog should not leap out of the car as soon as the door is opened.

Where you start the pup's initial training can have a considerable bearing on how quickly it will learn. Do not try and train it somewhere where there are distractions in the shape of other dogs, game scent, children playing ball and the like. It needs to be concentrating on you – and you on it – if either of you is to derive any benefit from the exercise. Much later on, when the basic lessons have been firmly established, training where there are distractions can be useful in teaching the pup that it must still obey orders, even when there is something more interesting that it would like to do, but in the early stages there is quite enough for it to think about just absorbing its first lessons.

Put your pup on the lead, tell it to 'sit' and gently pull back on the lead with one hand while pushing the dog's backside onto the ground with the other. Keep it there for a few seconds while repeating the command, then say 'heel' and walk off with the pup beside you. If it tries to race ahead check it gently but firmly and bring it back to your side while repeating the command 'heel'. Walk a few paces then say 'sit' and put the pup back into the sitting position. Then 'heel' and move off; 'sit' and stop again. And then again. Spend just a few minutes doing this and then give up before the pup gets bored.

Praise it and make a fuss of it. Carry a few dog biscuits in your pocket and give the dog one now and again if bribery seems to work.

Learning to 'sit' is one of the cornerstones of your pup's basic education.

Always give the 'heel' command before moving off from the sitting position. Beware of saying 'good dog' and then setting off. Dogs do not understand English. If they associate the sound of 'good dog' with getting up and walking away they will assume that 'good dog' means 'get on'. This could become a real problem later in their training.

Do not carry on with this or any other exercise for too long. Puppies have a short attention span and will soon get bored with constant repetition. A few minutes' lesson every day is a far better regime than a couple of hours once a week. The pup should enjoy the lessons, as should you. Neither of you should approach a lesson with the attitude that this is something unpleasant to be got over as quickly as possible. Always aim to end on a good note, praising the pup for getting it right, rather than telling it off for doing it wrong. If it starts to get stubborn and refuses to sit or pulls away from you on the lead, you have probably done more than enough for one lesson.

Once told to 'stay' your dog should not move until told.

After a while – it might be a couple of days or it might be a couple of weeks – your pup will be sitting automatically when you give the 'sit' command, and walking to heel on a loose lead. Since you are no longer having to hold the lead in one hand and push the pup down with the other you can begin to incorporate hand signals into its education.

Hand signals are particularly useful for shooting dogs. There will be times when you want to work your dog as quietly as possible – particularly if you use it for deer stalking for example – and times when the strength of the wind may be such that it cannot hear your voice or whistle. So each time you give the 'sit' command raise your free hand, with the palm towards the pup. It should soon come to associate the raised palm with the 'sit' command and to sit to the hand signal as readily as it does to your voice.

Now you can introduce your whistle into the game. Again, the idea is to give a signal on the whistle at nearly the same time as you give the 'sit' command. (If your pup is sitting to a hand signal you can do both together; if it still needs a voice command blow your whistle and then immediately say 'sit'). The dog should soon realise that a blast on the whistle means that it is about to be made to sit, and start doing it automatically.

Some handlers carry two whistles: one like the Acme Thunderer as a 'sit' or 'stop' whistle and another like the Acme 210½ for turn and recall. Others use a particular signal from their turn whistle to signify 'sit' – perhaps a single long blast which is easily distinguished from the staccato pips generally used for turn and recall. A Thunderer or its like has the advantage of being louder and quite distinct from the turn whistle, but too much noise may disturb game unnecessarily on a shoot day, besides which some shoots use three loud whistle blasts to signal the end of the drive. You will not be popular if you bring proceedings to a halt with the best of the birds yet to fly when all you wanted to do was to get your dog to sit.

The 'sit' and 'heel' are two parts of the training routine that are never redundant. A few sits and a little bit of heelwork to open a lesson establish that the pup is at work and under your command right from the off, and a couple of sits at the end of the session should ensure that you can finish, as you should always finish, with the pup being praised for getting something right. And however well the pup might seem to have learned these lessons in the quiet of the back garden, it will face a much sterner test when there is something to distract it, like a bolting rabbit or a running cock pheasant.

Once you are confident that the 'sit' has been firmly instilled you can begin to work on the 'stay'. Begin gently by sitting your pup and then, still holding the lead, stepping back a pace while holding your free hand up in the 'sit' command position and saying 'stay'. If it tries to follow you put it back to sitting in the original spot, tell it to 'stay' and step back again. At this stage always maintain eye contact with the pup, and only leave it for a few seconds. Then step back to it and praise it.

Some trainers will argue that the 'stay' command is unnecessary as the 'sit' command should mean 'Sit and stay sitting until I tell you to do otherwise.' I prefer to teach 'stay' as well as 'sit' as it can also be used when the dog is lying in the car for example, but if you think it is unnecessary, by all means dispense with it. The important thing is that your pup does not move off once it has been ordered to sit or to stay until it is given the next command to tell it to do so. Whether you opt to use the stay command or not you should gradually extend both the time and the distance between leaving your pup sitting and returning to it.

Until it is quite steady always return to it rather than calling it to you. If it breaks from its stay and rushes up to you do not punish it or tell it off, but do take it straight back to the original spot where it was left, sit it and repeat the 'stay' command. As with all lessons, a good maxim is to 'make haste slowly'. If you suddenly progress from asking your pup to 'stay' for thirty seconds while you are 2 yards away, to five minutes at 50 paces, it is only to be expected that it will feel insecure and come rushing to you for comfort.

The next stage is getting the pup to come to you when you call it or blow the recall whistle. Depending on your puppy and on what it has picked up while it was growing up this may be the easiest stage of its training – or it may be the hardest. You will already have a good idea which it is likely to be from the way it reacts when you call it. It may come racing to you, in which case the lesson is practically learned, or it may prefer to do its own thing and only come to hand when it suits. (If the latter is the case then you should be looking again at your relationship with the dog, particularly as regards which of you is the senior partner.) I trust that you will not have got into the habit of letting it off the lead and then spending the next twenty minutes trying to threaten, bribe or cajole it back into hand.

If your pup will not come back voluntarily then do not let it free in a situation where you will not be able to catch it up when you are ready. Play is more fun than work for dogs as well as for humans, and it is hardly surprising that they may prefer to carry on playing rather than to return when called. If all you do is to keep calling while your dog keeps ignoring you, it simply impresses on it that it does not have to listen unless it suits it.

All training is about repetition and habit. You keep repeating a command and enforcing the appropriate action from the dog until it obeys the command instinctively. And then you repeat it some more, and some more after that. Eventually it should reach the stage where it hears the 'sit' command and sits automatically – not because it has considered the alternatives and decided that there is not anything it would rather be doing right now, so it might as well sit, but because when it hears that word or that noise from the whistle, or sees that hand signal, 'sit' is what it does. Pronto. Without thinking about it.

Later on you are going to want it to obey that 'sit' command at the very moment that a rabbit bolts or a pheasant rises from under its nose. The fact that it will sit when it is walking at your side in a bare field with a lead round its neck and the prospect of a biscuit as reward does not mean that it will do it when it is 50 yards away with the scent and the sight of a rabbit filling its nostrils and catching its eyes. You have to keep reinforcing this lesson right through training and on into the dog's working life.

Refusing to come when called usually occurs because the pup has found something more interesting to occupy it. Do not try teaching the recall in a field full of rabbits or a park with other dogs playing. Find a quiet spot with no distractions and ensure that you have your dog's full attention with a few minutes' heel-work. Then sit the dog, tell it to stay, walk off a few paces and call

You should be confident that it will stay even when your attention is elsewhere: here concentrating on reloading a muzzle loader.

When it is away from you it must learn to return when you call it.

it to you with voice, whistle, gesture or whatever works best. Make a fuss of it when it arrives and then do it again, but not so often in one lesson that the pup becomes bored. Do not call it to you every time, leave it sitting and return to it at least as often as you bring it to you.

As training progresses gradually increase the distance at which the pup will still respond to your commands. It is one thing for it to sit when it is walking at heel, or to return to your side from 10 yards away, but it is quite another to get the same responses when it is galloping about at the far side of a field. Most dogs have a mental picture of the distance at which they feel under orders. Anywhere within that range means doing as they are told; anywhere beyond means that they feel they can safely ignore you. This may stem from a desire on the dog's part to challenge your authority, which means that it is deliberately ignoring you, or it may be that it has reached a distance at which it assumes that you are no longer addressing it.

In the case of deliberate disobedience one answer is to run towards the dog and repeat the command as you get nearer. A somewhat aggressive attitude will help initially, though as soon as the dog obeys it should be praised. Avoid these sorts of problems if possible by very gradually extending the distance at which you give commands. There is usually a break-through point when the pup suddenly realises that 'sit' means sit, whether it is right by your side or some distance away. You can usually tell from the dog's attitude whether it is being deliberately disobedient or simply ignoring a command because it thinks it does not apply to it. If it looks guilty when you approach it or takes care to keep well away from you then it is a fair bet that it heard you and chose not to obey. If it is clearly pleased to see you when you go up and rushes up with no qualms then it was probably disobeying out of ignorance rather than malice.

Never be tempted to skimp on the basics in order to press on to 'real' training. These early lessons are the most important part of its training. There is no substitute for a good, solid grounding in the simple things. If you skimp this part of your dog's education you will have problems right through your training regime and on during its working career. Most dogs are spoiled by trying to progress too quickly: very few because their trainers did not press on quickly enough.

The Next Steps

Once sitting, staying and walking to heel on a lead are thoroughly ingrained into the puppy you can gradually progress to the next

Walking to heel means staying close by, but not right in your pocket.

stages. Walking to heel while off the lead is a natural progression from heeling on a lead. The time to start this is when the pup is happily walking at heel on a loose lead. If it is still having to be constantly checked from pulling ahead or off to the side it is not ready to proceed without the lead. In any event, this is another lesson that should be introduced in a place where there are no distractions.

Start the lesson with the dog at your side, on the lead as normal. Walk a little way, do a couple of sits, then remove the lead, say 'heel' and walk on as normal, going a few steps then giving the 'sit' command just as if it was still on its lead. If it tries to pull away as it realises that it is no longer tied to you, repeat the 'heel' command while patting your thigh to encourage it to come in close again. This is a lesson better started in a confined space than in a wide-open field since if the dog does take off you can easily bring it back.

Always let the dog know that it is no longer 'at heel' when you end the lesson. Previously it will have known that it was free to run when you removed the lead. It is important that it does not get into the habit of just drifting off from heel. Finish by sitting it, then praise it and tell it it can 'get on'. It must still understand that it breaks from the sit only when released by a command from you.

So far the pup has only been told to sit while walking at your side. It now needs to learn to obey the sit command when some distance away from you. Begin by sitting it and telling it to stay, then walking away a few paces. Call the dog to you, and just as it arrives tell it to sit. Then progress by giving the sit command while it is still a few paces from you. If it is reluctant to stop before it reaches you try running towards it, repeating the command and with your hand raised in the 'sit' gesture. The dog should quickly get the message since it is not learning something new but simply obeying a command it already understands, albeit in a slightly different context.

If you have not already taught the dog to lie down on the 'down' command this can be introduced now in the same way as the 'sit' was taught, except of course that you will gently put the dog into a lying rather than a sitting position. Many gundog trainers use 'hup' as the command for 'lie down'. This is an abbreviation of an older command which I am told was either 'hold up' or 'muzzles up', the latter supposedly harking back to the days of muzzle-loading guns and the need to stop a dog from flushing more game while the gun was recharged. Either command will serve as long as you use it consistently.

You can introduce another hand signal at this stage if you wish; a downwards gesture made with the palm facing the ground is fine. Once the command has been mastered you should mix a few downs in with the sits when you are stopping the dog during the recall. It is still important that you return to the dog from time to time rather than always calling it to you.

Gradually extend the length of time the dog is staying and the distance you move away. Instead of keeping directly in front of it try walking off to one side, or circling around it. As it develops in confidence you can begin going out of its sight altogether, just for a few seconds at first and then for steadily lengthening periods. The dog may come after you at first; if so return it to the spot where it was left and repeat the 'stay' command. To begin with you should always return to the dog, or to within its sight before recalling it. Once it has mastered staying when you are out of sight you can begin calling it to come and find you.

Keep it simple at first: you should be no further away than just around the corner of the house or behind the nearest hedgerow. You are not teaching the dog to play hide and seek, you are teaching it to obey a command even if it cannot see the person giving that command. Lots of praise and a big fuss is the order of the day whenever it 'finds' you.

Basic Retrieving

Retrieving is not a skill that I would expect you to have to teach to a Labrador Retriever. The chances are that your pup will have been retrieving everything from shoes and socks to balls and sticks from the moment it was old enough to carry something in its mouth. It does, however, need to learn *when* to retrieve, and just as importantly, when *not* to retrieve. Provided that it is sitting, staying and coming to you when it is called the time has come to introduce it to controlled retrieving as opposed to picking up and fetching anything that takes its fancy.

The basic retrieving exercise is simple. Sit the dog at your side, tell it to stay and then throw the dummy, ball, dumb-bell, or whatever object it is that you want it to fetch. Make sure that it is steady, and then tell it to 'fetch it'. If yours is a typical Labrador it will race off and collect the dummy. Once the pup picks it up call it back to you and tell it to sit. Take the dummy and praise the dog, then bring it back to sitting at your heel.

As always, start with something simple and make sure that your dog has mastered it before moving on to more complicated exercises. The sitting delivery and the return to heel afterwards are pleasant icing on the cake but they are nowhere near as important as the fact that the pup has gone out and collected the dummy and brought it back to you in the first place.

It is unlikely with a Labrador, but if your pup should be reluctant to retrieve you can begin by letting it race after the dummy as soon as it is thrown and end by praising it lavishly as soon as it brings it back to you. If, as is more likely with a Labrador, it is only too anxious to please you by fetching anything and everything you can start it off with a more disciplined approach.

You will see that you are using the lessons that your pup has been learning over the past few weeks: the sit, the stay and the recall. It must learn only to go for a retrieve when you send it. Do not send it to collect the dummy every time you throw it. As an alternative, tell it to stay and then go and pick it up yourself. The pup must learn that it does not have an automatic right to retrieve every dummy that is thrown. Time spent now will be more than rewarded when temptations in the shape of grouse or pheasants are raining down all around your dog and you want to be sure that it will sit and stay until you tell it to do otherwise.

Training Classes

Dog-training classes are held all over the country and the chances are that, if you make enquiries, there will be one available somewhere near you. If you are lucky there may even be classes run specifically for gundogs, often with a professional gundog trainer as the tutor. Even if the classes are designed for more general training they can still be an excellent grounding for the beginner to gundog work.

You should ask about the syllabus before signing up for lessons. Some classes concentrate on 'ring craft', which means that they are primarily intended for people who want to compete in dog shows in the beauty classes and are therefore of little value to the working gundog owner. Others, however, will lean more towards 'obedience' and, if they follow the usual pattern that covers the requirements of obedience competitions, they will give you an excellent grounding in gundog training.

Obedience competitions require the dogs to walk to heel on and off their leads, to sit and drop on command, to stay with the owner out of sight for ten minutes or so, to retrieve a dummy, to be handled onto a particular spot in the competition ring, to retrieve one object from a number of similar ones using scent discrimination to identify it, and to accept commands such as 'sit', 'down' and 'stay' from a handler who is some distance away. In fact, everything required of a dog in an obedience competition is something that your Labrador will need to know if it is to be fully trained as a working gundog.

Beware of some of the nonsense that seems to be the current fashion in obedience competition, however. The last time I saw an organised obedience test all the dogs were walking 'at heel' with their muzzles actually touching the handler's left hip, and every retrieve was delivered with the dog virtually sitting on the handler's feet and pressing its chin into his stomach. 'At heel' for the working gundog means the dog staying close by your side, not trotting along with its nose in your trouser pocket, and I certainly do not want a wet, muddy or bleeding pheasant shoved against my best tweed shooting jacket. Besides, if the dog is supposed to be that close to you when it is at heel, how will you manage when you have two or three dogs all heeling at the same time?

Remember that attending a training class is not a substitute for training your dog. Training classes are primarily intended to teach owners how to train dogs. They are also useful for socialising your puppy: getting it used to meeting other dogs, to ignoring distractions from other handlers while still listening for your commands and learning that, for example, it is not its place to retrieve every dummy that is thrown. They also allow you to talk to other trainers, to compare progress with your puppies, perhaps to learn some new tricks of the trade. A good instructor may be able to save you a lot of time and trouble by showing you where you are going wrong, or by suggesting better ways to tackle problems when they arise. To many owners a weekly training class is as much a social event as a course of study, and some will attend for years. Attending classes certainly will not do your pup any harm and it might well do it a lot of good.

The early lessons – sitting, walking to heel, and coming to you on command – are in some ways the most difficult part of training because they are unnatural. They are not actions that the pup will perform instinctively, like picking up a stick and carrying it or chasing a rabbit. As such, they are actions that can take quite a time to perfect. Some more advanced aspects of training, such as blind retrieves or marking down fallen game, though they might seem much more complicated, are actually easier to teach because they involve the pupil in doing something that it would do of its own accord.

The early lessons also form the basis on which many of the others are built. When you are directing your dog onto a fallen bird you will use the 'sit' command to stop it and bring its attention on to you so that you can send it out, or left or right, or whatever is required. If you are working it in the beating line and there is a big bunch of pheasants just ahead of you, the recall command must overcome the dog's natural desire to rush forward and get amongst them and bring it back to your side, and then the heel command will keep it there until the birds have been flushed a few at a time to fly over the guns. The basic lessons do much more than introduce the dog to the concept of receiving and obeying orders: they lay the foundations for everything that follows. It is in both your interests to take plenty of time to ensure that those foundations are as solid as you can make them before you move on to the next stages of the pup's training.

4

Training for the Field

Perhaps the two greatest assets a trainer of dogs – or indeed, I imagine, of all animals – can possess, are patience and imagination, for I should say on these two qualities literally hang all the law and the prophets of training. – Lorna, Countess Howe
'Hounds and Dogs'
The Lonsdale Library 1943

All the work that we have done with the pup up to now has been designed to teach it the basic good manners that any dog should learn, whether it is intended to work as a shooting dog or just be a family pet. Only when the basics have become properly instilled can you move on to the more advanced aspects of its education. It is important, though, that you do not forget the simple exercises as you progress to the more interesting stuff. Walking to heel, sitting and staying should become part of the pup's normal routine when it is out for a walk, and they will always be useful ways to open a training session in order to set the mood for the work to come.

Before beginning to train your puppy for its real work in the shooting field it is worth giving some consideration to exactly what you hope to achieve at the end of the training. Visit a shoot anywhere in the country and watch the dogs at work. You may see dog work of the highest standard, or you may see dogs apparently running totally wild. You may well see both on the same shoot. Some owners will only be happy if their dogs are properly under control at all times, sit patiently by their peg until sent for a retrieve and never even think about running in. Others are just as happy to let the dog do its own thing, provided that it flushes a few pheasants, retrieves shot birds and turns up for its dinner at the end of the day.

I am exaggerating somewhat, but every shooting man will know examples of both types of owner, and both types of dog. And between these two extremes are all the other owners, trainers, handlers and dogs: some incredibly good, some hideously bad, but

Only you can decide the standard you will be happy to achieve.

most somewhere in between. I suspect that very few shooting men would actually *prefer* a dog that runs wild to one that is well behaved and under control, but at the same time the majority of guns will probably be more than content with a dog whose performance falls somewhat short of field trial standards, provided that it does its work efficiently and does not have any major faults such as a hard mouth.

Here we will be looking at training your Labrador as a beating dog – that is to say a dog that is used to flush game for the gun – as well as a retriever. We will be touching on various aspects of dog work that you may or may not wish to cover when you are training your own dog. If your intention is to work the dog only as a retriever then there is no point in training it to hunt live game in the beating line. All you will be doing is unnecessarily risking creating havoc with the training programme. By the same token, if all you want is a beating dog (and if so, why choose a retriever rather than a spaniel?) there is little sense in getting your youngster all fired up with the joys of retrieving and then denying it the

Waiting patiently by the peg for the chance of a retrieve.

opportunity. If what you want is a dog that will sit at your side while you shoot driven game, then pick up the birds around your peg at the end of the drive, then steadiness may be the most important part of your training. The ability to direct the dog onto a bird that has fallen a couple of hundred yards away across three fields, two hedges and an open ditch may not feature in your wish list at all. And if you want a rough shooting dog to hunt out game on a walked-up shoot and then retrieve it for you then you will be aiming for a combination of hunting ability and steadiness mixed with good retrieving skills. The important thing when you start to train a dog for work in the shooting field is to have a clear objective in your mind. You should decide what you want *your* dog to be capable of doing and work towards that end rather than wasting time and effort in trying to teach it tricks that you will not use in the shooting field. A dog that can do all that you require of it, and do it well, is far more useful in the field than one that has been half-trained to do everything, but tends to do most things badly.

That said, if you have the time, the right rapport with your dog, and a dog with the latent ability, there are few things more satisfying than working a well-trained and well-mannered Labrador, whether you are picking up, beating, rough shooting, wildfowling or perhaps dogging in poults around the release pens prior to the start of the shooting season. Good dog work is its own reward, for both dog and handler, and there is always a demand for the services of a well-trained dog.

Equipment

There is an enormous variety of gundog training equipment available through shops and mail-order outlets. Some of the items offered will be used by practically every trainer, others are of strictly limited – even dubious – value; but none of the many dog training aids and devices are actually essential in order for you to train your Labrador. A piece of string will do for a lead, an old pair of socks rolled up into a ball will do for a retrieving dummy, and your own lips can furnish the whistle. That said there are several items that are likely to be found in almost every retriever trainer's arsenal, and none of them will break the bank.

A lead should be an automatic part of any dog handler's everyday equipment. However good your dog is at sticking to your heel you should always have a lead to hand when you are out and about with it. You never know when you might need it. A bitch in heat will induce mutiny in all but the steadiest of dogs. That, a whistle – or a pair of whistles if you prefer – and some canvas dummies for retrieving practice form the basic requirements for the Labrador trainer.

I am inclined to believe that the choice of whistle is relatively unimportant, provided that you are consistent in the way you blow it. If you buy one of the branded products such as the Acme 210½ you will be able to replace it with an exact replica if you should ever lose it or break it. On the other hand, you are quite likely to find that some of the other handlers will be using exactly the same whistle, which can be confusing for the dog. Buying a stag-horn whistle or something of that nature will mean that you have a sound that is exclusive to your dog, but it also means that if you lose or break it you will not be able to get an exact replacement. That said, most dogs will adapt to a new whistle with little or no trouble once they have heard it a few times and begun to recognise it.

Whatever whistle you choose it is not a good idea to select one that is particularly loud. Not only does a loud whistle run the risk of scaring game – or appearing to the keeper to be scaring game, which may be just as important – but it draws attention to you, possibly at just the moment when you would prefer not to be in the limelight. The fact that you are frantically trying to call your

Always carry a lead – a piece of string will suffice . . .

. . . though this is probably rather more lead than is strictly necessary.

dog back in to heel is probably not something that you want to advertise to the rest of the beating line.

Besides the more conventional whistles, there is the option of the so-called 'silent' dog whistle, which is actually a whistle with a note so high pitched that it is virtually inaudible to humans, though still coming within a dog's hearing range. Some trainers claim miraculous properties for this whistle, but having tried one I found it no better than a normal one, with the added problem that at times I wondered whether it really was making a noise or not. With an ordinary whistle you will at least know for sure that you are giving out a clear signal, even if your dog appears not to be hearing it.

The standard retrieving dummy is a soft, canvas-covered cylinder with a short toggle on one end that acts as a carrying handle and a launcher to make it easier for you to throw it. The basic dummy can be supplemented by various specialist versions: heavier models designed to simulate retrieving a hare, lighter ones for use by puppies, special waterproof models and others covered in rabbit fur or the like. You can buy them in bright colours as well as the usual drab green, which may be handy if your pup fails to pick one after you have thrown it into cover and you have to search for it yourself. You can doctor an ordinary dummy by attaching a rabbit skin or a pair of pheasant wings to it in order to make retrieving a bit more interesting for your pup, and to introduce it to the taste and texture of game. And, as we have seen, you can make your own dummies out of practically anything that seems suitable for the pup to retrieve.

Manufactured dummies are the result of a lot of experience and experimentation, so if you do decide to make your own you would do well to be guided by their general specification. The tough, canvas outer covering makes them long-lasting and generally impervious to puppy teeth. They weigh about the same as a dead rabbit or pheasant, which both gets the pup used to the sort of load it will be expected to carry when it is working properly and is also a convenient weight for you to throw. The size and shape fits easily into a dog's mouth: not so long that one end will trail on the ground as it runs with it, nor so small that there is any danger of the pup swallowing it and choking.

Dummy launchers, which use a blank cartridge to propel the dummy, can be useful for getting the pup used to gunfire and to associating the sound of a shot with the prospect of a retrieve. A word of warning though: the sharp 'crack' made by blank ammunition is quite different from the sound of a shotgun and may actually be more distressing to some dogs. The same is true of blank-firing starting pistols. The starting pistol is a useful tool though, since it is obviously easier to carry one in your pocket when you are training your dog than to walk around with a shotgun over your arm. There are also limitations on where you are allowed to take a shotgun whereas, in theory, there are no such restrictions on starting pistols. A word of caution: if you use a starting pistol to train your dog in a public place such as a park there is a danger that a call to the police from some well-meaning member of the public may result in your being pounced on by an armed response unit. This is unlikely to be a pleasant experience for you or your pup.

A long line that you can attach to the dog's collar may prove useful for recalls and for allowing a pup limited freedom to run while still maintaining overall control. Keep a close watch if your pup is running 'free' while trailing a line because it is very easy for the line to become twisted around a leg, which could result in a serious injury. Flexi-leads, which have a spring-loaded recoil mechanism for rewinding the line save a lot of tangles and tripping over trailing lengths of string, though they do not allow the pup to run 'free' while trailing the line behind it – a practice actually more commonly encountered in pointer and setter training than in the schooling of Labradors.

There are all kinds of leads and collars on the market, ranging from a simple length of rope with a loop in the end to special quick-release collars and leads based on the design of those used by the slipper at coursing meetings. Some people swear by choke chains for teaching heelwork; others condemn them as cruel and unnecessary. Spiked collars – metal collars made with blunt spikes on the inside – are available to curb a really dedicated puller, though they should never be needed by the Labrador trainer who has concentrated properly on heelwork at the start of his pup's education. Incidentally, it is never advisable to allow a dog to work in any sort of cover or to cross fences while wearing a collar in case it becomes snagged and traps or injures the dog.

Electric collars – radio-controlled devices designed to allow the handler to give the dog an electric shock from a distance – are now legally approved for use in the United Kingdom and are widely available. This is a controversial subject: the electric collar is championed by some trainers while being soundly condemned for its cruelty by others. In the interests of research I have actually experimented with one and found that at its lowest setting it produced no more than a mild tingle, while at higher levels the 'shock' was just that – a very considerable shock. That said, I do not think it was as painful as a sharp clip across the backside with a lead or a whippy stick would be (I did not experiment with those), and the pain went away as soon as the shock ceased.

Although referred to as 'training collars' it should be emphasised that they are *not* a magic method of training a dog with no real effort on the part of the trainer. If you cannot train a dog without an electric collar then you are not going to train it with one. All that an electric collar does is allow you to administer punishment to the dog when it is at a distance from you. Unless it knows why it is being punished the most likely result from using an electric collar is to cow the dog and possibly make it more difficult to train. They can, however, occasionally be invaluable as a possible cure for certain serious faults such as chasing farm stock, where failure to break the habit may mean the dog will have to be put down.

More Retrieving

Simple retrieving, where the pup watches a dummy being thrown and then is sent to collect it, is only the beginning of the most important part of its training. There will be times when it *is* able to see a bird fall and then go straight out to collect it, but unless its shooting work is very limited it must be able to do much more than that. It must learn to mark the fall of game, to see several birds shot in succession and to remember where each one fell, and to hunt for birds even when it has not seen anything fall. To this end it will need to practise blind retrieves and multiple retrieves, and learn to follow directions from the handler. It should learn to retrieve from water, and from across water, and it will need to become accustomed to the sound of gunfire. If you intend to use your pup as a rough-shooting dog, or in the beating line, it will also have to learn to hunt free while remaining under your control.

Take care not to make the puppy stale during this part of its training. Retrieving should be a treat, not a chore, and should never be allowed to become boring. Once the pup has mastered the basics you can make things more interesting by throwing the dummy into cover so that it will have to search for it instead of being able to see it at the fall. Encourage it with 'hi lost' or whatever command you plan to use to tell it there is a bird to be picked while it is searching. Keep things simple at first and avoid sending it in to a bunch of stinging nettles or thick brambles. It still should not be fetching every dummy you throw: leave it to sit on some retrieves and go and fetch them yourself.

As the dog progresses you can add more dummies, building up from one to two, then three or four so that it begins to learn to mark and remember the fall of more than one at a time. Start

Labradors can work as beaters as well as pickers up.

slowly; do not attempt to go straight from single, seen retrieves to expecting it to mark and retrieve four dummies scattered in different directions in thick cover. As it learns to work with more than one dummy you can also begin to teach it the rudiments of direction. Throw one off to the left and another to the right and then start the pup towards the one that you threw first. Point it in the direction you want it to go and then set it off with a wave of your arm in the right direction. If it turns towards the wrong dummy stop it with a 'sit' command and then direct it to the right one, perhaps going with it part of the way to ensure that it understands what you require. Take the dummy from it once it has collected it, and then set it off with another wave towards the second one. With practice it will begin to associate the wave of your hand not just with which dummy to fetch, but also with the direction in which it should go to find the dummy. Eventually the response to your hand signals should become automatic, and you will be able to send the dog left or right, even if it has not seen a dummy thrown first.

Vary the exercise by telling the pup to stay and going away from it before throwing the dummies. Keep it simple at first, perhaps just throwing a single dummy in such a direction that, if the dog does yield to the temptation to run in before it is ordered to, it will have to pass you to reach the retrieve thus giving you the chance to stop it and correct it before it collects the dummy. As you become more confident you can throw the dummy off to the sides or even back over its head. When sending the dog back you can introduce the command 'back' or 'go back' as well as another hand signal such as an arm raised high above your head and thrust forward in a pushing motion.

Always insist on steadiness, and take your dog back and make it stay if it breaks from the sit before it is released by your command. Always proceed at a pace that suits your pup, not according to some timetable that you have dreamed up or to meet a particular date such as the start of the shooting season. If it is having problems understanding what you want it to do then stop. Go back to something easier and then build up its confidence over the next few lessons before you try the exercise again.

You can mix up the work even more now, throwing several dummies and collecting one or two of them yourself and then sending the pup to collect those that are left. Vary the type of retrieve by sometimes dropping a dummy as you walk along instead of throwing it and then sending the dog back to collect it. Use 'go back', reinforced by the hand signal. Let the dog see you drop the dummy at first until it is used to being sent back, then vary the exercise further by planting a dummy unseen and then sending it to search for it. In effect you are introducing it to three different types of retrieve: one where it has seen a dummy fall and can go to the spot from where it is sitting; one which involves remembering where a dummy was dropped and then going back to collect it; and, probably the most difficult to grasp, going to look for a retrieve even though it has not seen a dummy thrown or dropped.

With the 'left', 'right' and 'back' commands added to the recall command, coupled with the ability to get the pup to sit from a distance, you have all the tools in place to enable you to handle it onto an unseen retrieve. This part of the training can save you a great deal of walking when you have progressed to real work and the dog has to be sent off into the distance to collect a bird which has towered or flown well away before dropping. Beware of making the dog too reliant on you to put it right on the spot when you are handling it on to a distant retrieve. It is far better to place it a few yards downwind of the spot and then encourage it to hunt out the dummy. Although you may know precisely where you placed the dummy when setting up a blind retrieve in training, you will not have the same degree of control when you are working on a shoot. A dog that can not only listen to and obey orders, but can also think for itself, is far more use than one which has to

Most Labradors love water and take to it naturally.

rely entirely on *your* judgement in order to find a shot bird.

Most Labradors love water and will plunge in at any opportunity, particularly in hot weather. If your pup is typical of the breed introducing it to retrieving from water may require nothing more than throwing a dummy into a pond or stream and allowing it to fetch it. Start in the shallows and get the pup used to the idea of picking a dummy from just a few inches of water before asking it to get out of its depth and swim to it. In the unlikely event that it dislikes the water you will have to proceed very gently, building up its confidence a little at a time. It may help if you get into the water with it, either in your wellington boots or even going for a swim yourself, and calling the dog to join you. Choose a warm day – particularly if you are going to go swimming – and encourage the pup just to paddle about at first. Retrieving can come later when its confidence has grown enough for it to swim voluntarily. Do not even think about throwing it into a deep pool to 'make it learn': you might well put it off water for life.

If you have an older dog, or a friend with a well-trained retriever, try taking both dogs out occasionally and keeping your pup sitting while the other dog collects some retrieves. It is important to emphasise to the pup that it does not have automatic rights to every dummy that is thrown; otherwise, once you start working it, it is liable to take the same proprietary attitude to every bird that falls. While it may stay quite happily while you go and collect a dummy the sight of another dog fetching 'its' retrieve is much more likely to make it break away. It is much easier to set up the situation during training when your full attention is on the dog than to try and cope with it out in the field on its first day shooting in company.

Retrieving lessons should never go on and on until both of you are fed up with the game. It is always better to stop while the pup is still keen to go on than to carry on to the point where it is bored and wants to give up. As long as it looks forward eagerly to its retrieving work it makes introducing some of the more advanced lessons that much easier.

Multiple Roles

We touched on several of the 'advanced' lessons already in the last section. The amount of time and effort you will need to put into some of these exercises will depend on the type of work you have in mind for your dog. If you are planning to use it only for picking up then the emphasis will obviously be on the various retrieving skills, whereas the dog whose main function will be in the beating line or flushing game on a rough shoot will need more emphasis on hunting.

Many Labradors, however, will be expected to become jacks of all trades, picking up shot birds or sitting beside their owners on a driven shoot one day and working live birds out of cover on another. Indeed, on many shoots, where the guns and the beaters swap roles on alternate drives, their dogs are expected to switch from picker up to flushing dog and back again several times in a day.

This can be a terribly confusing business for the dogs. Consider it from their point of view. On the first drive of the day they sit by their owner's peg and remain there until the end of the drive. Then they are sent to retrieve the shot game. A winged pheasant that runs from the dog should be pursued, caught and carried back to the boss; a pricked bird tucked under a bush should be picked and similarly returned. And then it is the boss's turn to be a beater and instead of sitting quietly beside him the dog has to forge ahead (though not too far ahead) and hunt. And when it does discover a pheasant tucked under a bramble, or running off through the wood ahead of it it *must not* catch it and carry it back to the boss. This time it has to press it until it flies and then leave it and get on with hunting for the next one.

If it is sent to retrieve a wounded bird it is expected to get its nose down on the bird's foot scent and follow it up until it catches the bird. In the beating line a dog that follows foot scent will often end up boring straight through the drive on the heels of a running pheasant and draw the wrath of the keeper for getting too far ahead of the line. Is it any wonder that dogs get confused when they are praised for fetching a bird at one moment and then told off for doing what to them is exactly the same thing a few minutes later? Switching between picking up and beating is far from easy, particularly when birds are sitting so tightly that it is easy for the dogs to peg them.

It makes things considerably easier all round if you plan to use your pup only for retrieving or only for beating, but the Labrador is versatile enough to do both if you require. We will look more closely at the particular problems associated with asking the dog to play multiple roles when we consider his introduction to the shooting field proper.

Steadiness

By nature a dog is a hunter and its natural instinct is to run down and catch prey. Take any dog out to a field where there are rabbits or hares and, given the opportunity, it will chase them. While chasing fur may be a harmless fun for a family pet and a positive virtue in a greyhound or lurcher, it is taboo for the shooting dog. A dog chasing a rabbit is a dog out of control and worse: there is a very real danger that it may get shot. It happens all too easily: a rabbit bursts from cover, the nearest gun swings on to it with all his attention on the rabbit and does not see the pursuing dog until too late. Chasing fur or feather is an unnecessary indulgence and a dangerous practice in a working gundog.

However, there will be times when we *want* a dog to chase its quarry. A pheasant that has been brought down with a broken wing, but no other serious injuries, can run like a stag, and to make a successful retrieve the dog is going to have to run after it. Even worse from the trainer's point of view are those pheasants that prefer running to flying when disturbed by the beating line. Particularly towards the end of the season, the only way to get a wily cock pheasant off his feet and into the air may be for the dog to press him hard enough to force him to 'fly or die', and again, this effectively means chasing him until he takes off.

About to hunt out a wood, this Labrador can revert to its retrieving role at the end of the drive.

So we have a dilemma. We want the dog to curb its natural instinct to chase – except sometimes, when we want it to indulge itself to the full.

The first thing to do is to stop your dog from chasing. You should already have set the ground rules for this part of its training by making it remain at the sit while you are throwing dummies for it to retrieve. The dog's natural instinct is to race off as soon as the dummy is thrown but hopefully, by now, it will be reining in its enthusiasm and waiting for the command to 'fetch'. Now we want to take that discipline a step further and teach it to sit and stay sat as soon as it sees a rabbit bolt or a pheasant fly.

The temptation here is far greater than when you were teaching the pup to retrieve. First, a bolting rabbit with its scent and flashing white scut bobbing along is a far more alluring prospect than a canvas dummy being tossed through the air. Worse, for the retrieve the pup was sitting close by your side and under your direct control at the moment of temptation – and you could decide when to throw the dummy, perhaps having first emphasised your requirements with the 'stay' command. You do not have the same control over the moment when a rabbit will run or a bird will fly. When the dog bolts a rabbit or flushes a pheasant it is going to be up on its feet and on the move and quite possibly some little distance from you as well as being excited by the scent of game in its nostrils. Is it any wonder that it wants to chase?

Before even thinking about introducing the pup to the delights and temptations of live game you should be very confident of its instant obedience to the 'sit' command. If it will not sit to order when it is just wandering along at your heel it is not going to obey the command when its every instinct is telling it to get on and catch the rabbit or hare that has just exploded from under its nose. Even if it is absolutely reliable on the 'sit' command it may still forget everything it has been taught when it first encounters game at close quarters.

It may, of course, already be quite familiar with game, particularly if you live in an area where rabbits, hares, partridges or pheasants are likely to be encountered when it is being exercised. If so it is quite likely that it will have experienced the delights of a good chase. If nothing else this will probably have sharpened its enthusiasm for hunting, but now it must learn that chasing is forbidden.

A professional trainer will probably have access to a rabbit pen for this part of the pup's training. Unless you are lucky enough to know of someone who will allow you to use their pen you are going to have to make do with whatever is available locally. This can be any field that has a supply of rabbits or other game where you have permission to take your puppy. The training is essentially nothing more than letting the pup bolt a rabbit or flush a pheasant (or simply see a rabbit bolting or pheasant flushing) and making it sit as soon as it happens. Then you repeat the exercise until it is sitting automatically.

This sounds quite simple in theory. In practice the dog may grasp this part of its training in a few lessons or may require weeks of work.

Unless you are very, very confident that your pup will sit to command whatever the temptation I would suggest that you start this part of its training with a lead or a line. Take the dog into a field where you expect there to be rabbits (or into the rabbit pen if you are so blessed) and walk it along until it sees a rabbit bolting. Then give a 'sit' command, by voice or whistle, and make sure that it does sit. If it tries to chase you can check it with the line and then repeat the command and enforce it. Praise the dog, keep it sitting until it has calmed down, and then go and find another rabbit to repeat the exercise.

You do not have to wait until something is actually flushed before making your pup sit. It will probably be excited at the prospect of finding game and may be a little deaf as a result. Make it sit from time to time even when there are no rabbits running or pheasants flying. It should stay at the sit until you either tell it to get on or call it back in to heel. As well as sitting to flush it will also get the idea that it hunts only as long as you want it hunting; it doesn't automatically get to run on until the whole wood or field has been cleared and the fence brings it to a halt.

As ever, do not overdo it and try to end on a positive note; praise the pup for a simple sit performed walking at heel rather than scolding it for yet another attempt to chase. Once it is sitting without having to be physically checked by the line you can give it a little more freedom. Let it trail the line, but keep it close by you so that you have a chance to grab the line if it does respond by chasing. Eventually you should be able to dispense with the line altogether. The aim is, through repetition, to produce an automatic reaction from the dog of sitting as soon as it sees game away.

Hunting

The way in which you want your Labrador to hunt will depend on the type of work for which you plan to use it. If you are going to be working it on a rough shoot to flush game you will need to accustom it to a hunting pattern that keeps it within 20 yards or so of you. It is no use if it gets its nose on the scent of a running cock pheasant and flushing it 100 yards ahead of the guns. In the beating line too you will want the dog to stay reasonably close and hunt out the cover thoroughly rather than charging off through the woods on the track of a running pheasant. Alternatively, if you are going to use it only as a picking-up dog you will want it to be quite confident of getting out and away from you when it has to track a winged bird across the fields. Another dilemma.

Steadiness to flush is less important in a dog that is used only for retrieving since its job is not to hunt game unless it has been shot and killed or wounded. However, it should still be taught not to chase fur, nor to take off in pursuit of any unshot game that it might flush while it is hunting for dead and wounded birds. Such temptations are inevitable when working on the shoot and basic good manners demand that your dog should be steady.

The work you have been doing to teach your pup steadiness to game will also have had the incidental effect of encouraging it to hunt. There is a school of thought that says you should beware of restricting the distance at which you allow a young dog to hunt during training in case it becomes reluctant to leave your side later when you want it to get well out for a retrieve. In my experience it is a lot harder to rein in a dog which is used to getting well out than it is to encourage a dog to get out after it has been accustomed to hunting in a close pattern. I would strongly suggest that you keep your pup well within your ken during this early hunting experience and worry about getting it farther out later. You are more likely to find that it needs keeping in once you start shooting with it than that it has to be pushed farther out.

A word of caution. The Labrador was bred as a retrieving dog. An instinct to hunt by quartering the ground in the manner of a spaniel was not one of the characteristics for which the breeders of the early Labradors were selecting. If you are expecting your pup to hunt with the drive and enthusiasm of a Springer Spaniel you are likely to be disappointed. However, you can still train your dog to hunt with a decent pattern and encourage it to investigate the most likely patches of cover on its beat. Some Labradors love hunting and take to it with all the enthusiasm of a spaniel, but others may be reluctant to crash through brambles and nettles unless there is the encouragement of some game scent to drive them on. This keenness to hunt is just something that your pup may or may not have.

All gundogs locate game by using their noses. The scent of the game is carried to them on the wind. If the dog passes upwind of a bird it will not find it unless there is ground scent to lead it to the quarry. It follows therefore that your dogs will have the best chance of finding game when you work them into the wind. On a grouse moor with a pointer or setter it may be practical to arrange things so that the dog's beat is always into the breeze, but it is unlikely that you can do this on a driven shoot where the coverts may have to be beaten in a particular direction irrespective of the quarter from which the wind is blowing.

On the other hand, on the grouse moor the guns will be relying absolutely on the pointing dogs to find game for them. Any coveys that are missed by the dogs will probably sit tight and let the shooting party walk right past them. In a beating line there will be other dogs hunting the cover as well as beaters tapping with their sticks to get the pheasants into the air. Often the aim of the keeper will be to drive the birds through the covert to a flushing point and obviously birds running ahead of the line will be leaving any amount of foot scent behind them as they go. At times the job of dogs in a beating line is as much to keep herding the game forward and prevent birds from breaking back as it is to actually find and flush them.

The usual way to teach a dog to quarter its ground is to hunt it (into the wind initially) while setting the quartering pattern you want it to follow. With your Labrador, as with a spaniel, that pattern is likely to be just a few yards either side of you: with a bird dog the range may eventually be several hundred yards on either flank. Be glad that you are training a Labrador and not an Irish Setter.

Set the pattern by sending the dog off to one side, across the wind, and then turning it and bringing it back once it has gone the required 20 yards or so. The usual signal for 'turn' is two or three sharp pips on the whistle but initially you can call it with your voice or use your recall signal on the whistle. As it comes back to you send it on across your front to hunt out on the opposite side, then turn it again and bring it back across in the original direction.

If the dog is too keen and tends to race on too far on each cast you can attach a line to its collar and tug it round each time you blow the turn whistle. As it starts to respond progress to letting it drag a loose line behind it. This gives it the illusion that it is still under tight control and will give you a chance of catching the line as it crosses and giving it a sharp reminder if your dog is starting to pull too far on each cast. If you are working the dog on a line you will have to find an open area with no bushes or trees or the line will constantly be snagged.

Another method is to start the pup off to one side by walking in that direction yourself and encouraging it to run ahead. Then, as soon as it is on the move, turn and set out in the opposite direction, calling it back to you and then sending it on ahead again as it reaches you. Seeing you walking away is a powerful incentive to most pups to come and join you. Proceed across the field in a series of zigzags until the dog starts to quarter of its own accord.

This is really spaniel work, not retriever work. Beaters working in woods or game crops are generally content if their dogs will stay within a reasonable distance and investigate any likely bits of cover on their part of the beat. Particularly on drives where there may be several hundred – even several thousand – pheasants in one covert it is more important that your dog should be under control than that it should find every last pheasant in the wood. Nevertheless, if you take the time to train your pup to work a decent pattern you will have a better dog than one that just mills about aimlessly.

Unless the major part of your shooting involves the dog hunting for game rather than retrieving it you should consider strictly limiting the amount of hunting that your dog is allowed during its first season or two. Indeed, many trainers would make a strong

Shooting grouse over a pointer, with the guns relying absolutely on the dog to find game.

case for not allowing it to hunt free at all until you are absolutely confident in its steadiness at retrieving work. We will return to this subject in chapter 5.

Gunfire

The first thing to establish is that you *do not* test for gun-shyness by firing a gun over the pup's head. The only thing that such idiocy is likely to achieve is to make the dog gun-shy.

The sound of the gun should be introduced gradually. Keith Erlandson, one of the most successful and most experienced gundog trainers of the past thirty years, advocates starting with a blank firing pistol and then progressing via a four-ten and a twenty-bore to the full report of a twelve-bore. Excellent though the advice is, it may not be practical for your particular circumstances if you do not have access to such a variety of weapons – and such access is becoming increasingly restricted as police forces try to cut down on the number of weapons that are held by shooting enthusiasts.

You can accustom your pup to sudden noises from an early stage by clapping your hands, rattling its dinner bowl, letting it hear the sound of shots from the television and the like, though the introduction to a real gunshot should be left until it is well on its way to adulthood – probably nine months or more. Take the pup out into a field, well away from buildings or the edges of woodland that can cause an echo and magnify the sound of the shot. A windy day helps to minimise the sound, though obviously the wind should be blowing the sound away from the pup. If you can press a friend into helping with this exercise then so much the better.

If you can arrange things so that a shot is fired some distance away while the pup is playing you can get a first indication of how it is likely to react. In most cases it will do little more than raise its head and look to see what caused the sudden noise. Provided that it doesn't seem cowed, or worse, scuttle back with its tail between its legs, you can gradually introduce the sound of shots into its life.

Sit the pup and send your friend at least 100 yards away, depending on the size of gun you are using. If you only have a twelve-bore make that 200 yards, and of course, send him down wind. If you are on your own, sit the pup and tell it to stay, then retreat the requisite distance yourself. Fire a single shot and watch the dog's reaction.

If you are lucky, it will do no more than prick up its ears. If you have a friend firing the shots you can make a fuss of the pup and tell it what a good dog it is: perhaps reward it with a biscuit or some other little treat. Try another shot or two, getting a little nearer each time and then stop. You should not keep getting closer and closer until the pup becomes nervous. If you are on your own call the pup to you after firing a shot and praise and reward it. All being well you can gradually progress to the point where you can fire your starting pistol or shotgun in the pup's immediate vicinity with no adverse reaction. At this stage you can incorporate a shot into your retrieving practice so that your pup associates the sound of the gun with the likelihood of something to retrieve.

Note that I said 'all being well'. If the pup does show signs of nervousness at the sound of gunfire do not continue the exercise in the hope that it will 'get used to it'. It is more likely to become increasingly nervous. Stop and wait until another day, then try again with the gun farther away. Take a pocketful of treats to try to get it to associate the sound of a distant shot with something

There may be times in the beating line when you will be asked to keep your dog close by you.

pleasant. If you or a friend have an older dog that is used to gunfire you could let your young dog romp with it while the distant shots are being fired. You can try getting someone to fire a distant shot while the pup is hunting rabbits or chasing a ball – anything that will make it associate the sound of a shot with pleasure instead of fear. And progress slowly; this is not a part of training that you can rush.

Nervousness caused by the sound of shots can sometimes be alleviated by time and patience, though it is said that a dog that is genuinely gun-shy may be impossible to cure. This is another instance where the owner/trainer whose working dog is also the family pet may wish to persevere long beyond the stage at which a professional trainer would have written the pupil off as a working gundog and started looking for a home for it with a falconer, or with a family with no interest in shooting. You can also probably afford to spend a lot more time trying to cure the problem than would be practical for a busy professional trainer with a lot of other dogs making demands on his time.

With any luck, though, your pup will take the introduction to gunfire in its stride, particularly if it is descended from a line of working dogs. Gun-shyness can be inherited as well as induced, and clearly your pup is less likely to have inherited such a problem if it is descended on both sides from working parents.

Retrieving Game

At some stage you will have to make the switch from retrieving dummies to retrieving real game. This should not be an abrupt transition but a gradual introduction. It is possible that your pup will already have encountered 'game' of some kind by this time, picking up the odd dead rabbit or small bird. It may even have picked the odd live rabbit, particularly if there has been an outbreak of myxomatosis in the area where you exercise it, though this is something to avoid if at all possible.

The pup should be started on cold game, which means something that has been dead for at least a day. If you have year round access to your shoot you may be able to shoot rabbits, pigeons, crows and the like whatever the time of year and so have a supply of retrieving material available to hand. If not you can store pigeons, rabbits or other game in feather (or in fur) in your freezer and take them out as you require them. Thaw them out before using them: the term 'cold' game should not be taken too literally. Beware of keeping dead game for too long, especially during warm weather. If it starts to get 'high' your pup may decide to eat it instead of retrieving it.

If you are using pigeons, which are very loose-feathered, as an introduction to real retrieving, you can wrap them in an old stocking initially. This will save the young dog from getting a mouthful of feathers which it may find unpleasant when it makes its first proper retrieve, but will still allow it to get the feel and scent of a dead bird rather than a canvas dummy. Proceed exactly as you do with a dummy: sit the dog, throw the game and then send the dog to collect it. Mix the odd 'real' retrieve in with retrieves on dummies, and remember to keep collecting some of the birds yourself to emphasise that it does not have the right to collect every bird that falls: it should only retrieve when you tell it to retrieve.

In some cases the pup may lose interest in dummies once it has started retrieving the real thing, though this would be quite unusual in a Labrador. If this should occur you can usually get round the need for an endless supply of cold game for retrieving practice by covering your dummies in rabbit skin or attaching some pigeon or pheasant wings to them using strong rubber bands. Though it is a nuisance, such a loss of interest on artificial retrieving objects is not something to worry about as long as the dog is still as keen as ever when it is sent for a retrieve on cold game.

The transition from cold game to 'real' retrieving on freshly shot fur or feather is dealt with in chapter 5.

Jumping

The ability to get over, under or through various types of fencing and other obstacles is an essential requirement for the majority of working Labradors. Game does not always drop conveniently on your side of the fence. A running pheasant can cross any number of boundaries and, unless you are going to follow along yourself and lift the dog across each one, you will need a dog that can get over them itself. A Labrador is not the lightest of dogs to manhandle over a fence: I once spent three weeks off work with a slipped disc after helping a reluctant jumper over some pig netting. Besides, a wet Labrador plastered in mud and clarts is not a pleasant burden, nor is it good for your best tweed shooting coat.

Some pups will need no introduction to jumping fences, quickly becoming adept at wriggling under, pushing through or jumping over whatever obstacle is in their path. This is a mixed blessing, especially when they start escaping from their run or from your garden. Others are typically wimps, running up and down with a worried expression on their faces when confronted with any obstacle over a foot high. Ideally you should aim for a dog that *can* clear a fence when ordered, but will not feel the urge to clear every fence it meets 'just because it's there'.

Do not start this part of the pup's training until it is at least nine months old. Jumping can cause damage to young bones and joints, particularly if your pup is a little on the heavy side. As with all training, start with something simple, not with a metre-high stock fence topped with two strands of barbed wire. A low fence, a hurdle or a couple of planks will serve nicely. Make sure that whatever you use is solid enough not to collapse if the pup puts its weight on it as it scrambles across it. A scare at this stage could put it off jumping for life. If you do not have a suitable low gate or fence for this early practice, make something up in the garden.

Encourage the pup to hop across, giving the command 'over'. You will find it more willing to jump across if you are on the other side of the fence and calling it to you rather than sending it away from you. Praise it when it gets it right and as always, do not overdo things. As it becomes more confident you can increase the height slowly and vary the type of fence.

The command 'over' in this context means get across the fence, hedge, stone wall or ditch by whatever means is most suitable – it does not necessarily mean go over the *top* of the obstacle. There is no point in the dog trying to clear a 4 ft (1 m) thorn hedge if it can

The ability to jump is useful, but always remember that barbed wire can inflict a nasty injury.

It is often better to eliminate the risk of injury by finding other ways for your dog to cross a fence.

just as easily squeeze through the bottom. Some handlers seem to have an obsession about making their dogs jump over every obstacle in their path regardless of any danger. There are times – when confronted with a rickety dry-stone dyke topped with a couple of strands of barbed wire for example – when it is safer for the dog (and for the wall) if you detour to find a gateway or lift the dog across. Some very nasty injuries can occur when dogs just fail to clear barbed wire fences, or when they get a leg twisted in between two strands of wire. Use the 'over' command when you are parting the strands of wire for the dog to step through a fence, or lifting the netting so that it can wriggle under it as well as when you want it to jump.

If you are concerned about your dog being injured when it jumps a fence topped with barbed wire, you can spread your coat or perhaps your game bag along the top strand and then get the dog to cross where the barbs are hidden. This can be a little hard on the lining of your coat, and has the obvious disadvantage that you can only protect your dog if you are right there at the point where it has to cross the fence. If it is three fields away in pursuit of a runner there is not a lot you can do to help it, short of running across the fields after it.

When you consider the youngster's jumping to be sufficiently competent you can start to introduce it into its retrieving exercises. Initially, throw a dummy over a fence or wall and then send the dog to collect it, giving the command 'over' as it reaches the fence. Later you can vary this by planting a dummy behind the obstacle and sending the dog for a blind retrieve. Take particular care if you work your dogs in country where there are dry-stone dykes. The weight of a Labrador bouncing across a dyke may be enough to tumble some of the stones out of the wall, or even collapse part of it altogether. If this happens you should do your best to replace the stones before moving on. Better still, if a wall looks at all fragile, do not let your dog jump it: find a gap or a gate.

Teaching Versus Learning

The time is now approaching when your pupil will be ready for its introduction to a real shooting situation – a subject we will consider in considerable detail in chapter 5. The transition from pupil to working dog, though, is considerably more complicated than simply taking it out on a shooting day and letting it turn its lessons into practice. There is a difference between what you can teach it and what it has to learn from practical experience in a shooting situation.

However good your pup has become at the various exercises you have been using in training, it still has a lot to learn – and 'learn' is the operative word. You can teach it manners and discipline: you can teach it to sit and to stay, to quarter the ground when it is hunting and to obey your hand signals from a distance. You can teach it not to run in to collect a retrieve, to sit when a rabbit bolts or a pheasant flies, to walk to heel and to stay in the car until it is told to get out. You have to teach it these things because in most cases they go against its natural inclinations. Left to itself your dog would chase anything it flushed and charge in to retrieve as soon as you tossed a dummy. Without instruction it would never learn to walk to heel or to sit when you raised your hand.

These things are *taught*. Once the dog starts to work properly there are a number of other things that it must *learn*. You can point it at a rhododendron bush, but it will have to learn to tell from the scent whether there is a pheasant lurking under it. You can send it to collect a runner but you cannot show it how to follow its scent across a ploughed field, through a ditch and into the next wood in order to retrieve it. It has to find out by experience the differing scents of grouse, woodcock, snipe, pheasant, partridge, duck, goose, rabbit, hare, pigeon and whatever else it may be required to hunt or retrieve, and to distinguish these scents from those of mice and voles, larks and sparrows and all the other creatures that it should simply ignore when it is at work.

It is only practical experience that will teach it not to hunt a heel scent – that is, not to track a bird in the direction it has come from rather than the way it is going. It will have to learn to thrust itself into thick cover in order to collect a wounded pheasant that has tucked itself tightly away, and to swim after a winged duck that keeps diving out of reach on the flight pond or in the tide. It needs experience to learn to track a wounded bird and stick to it even though other, undamaged birds may cross the scent and distract it. It needs to learn to get out and hunt for any birds that may be left behind the guns at the end of a drive even though it has not seen them fall. And it must learn that there will not be a bird to retrieve every time a shot is fired.

All these things can only come with experience. Until the dog goes shooting with you it cannot develop that sixth sense that some dogs seem to possess which tells them when a bird has been hit, even though it has shown no signs of damage. It has to learn to distinguish a wounded bird from one that is merely sitting tightly because it is exhausted after a flight. It has to learn to find game by air scent and by ground scent, and to distinguish between the foot scent of the bird that was feeding here an hour ago and that of the one that has just run off through the covert. In short, now that it is about to graduate from school it has to start to apply everything that it has been taught in order that it can begin to learn what its real job is all about.

5

Introduction to the Shooting Field

The quickest way to ruin a gundog is to take it shooting.
– Guy Wallace.

'The Versatile Gundog'
Swan Hill Press

However long and careful your training programme has been there must eventually come a time when you decide that your pup is ready to be introduced to the real thing. You will have spent weeks or perhaps months teaching it to sit and to stay, to walk at heel, jump fences, retrieve dummies from every conceivable sort of cover and sit instantly at the merest glimpse of a bolting rabbit or a flushing pheasant. Now you are going to take it out to do at least some of these things for real, on a shooting day, under battle conditions. The next few hours will see the result of all that hard work being put to use at last.

The next few hours may also see the dog irrevocably headed down the road to ruin. If I had a pound for every gundog, however meticulously trained, that was ruined on its first day shooting I would have no need to be writing this book.

I am exaggerating slightly of course – but only slightly. It is entirely possible, given the wrong type of temperament in the dog combined with some unfortunate circumstances on the first day of shooting, to ruin a dog in a single day, but it is more likely that the good habits so carefully inculcated through months of hard work will be broken over a few weeks. But they will still broken during the *first* few weeks.

There are two reasons for this. The first and probably the most common cause of a dog forgetting its manners, its lessons, and everything else it has been taught, during its first few trips to the shoot is that it simply was not ready to be started on live game. There is a world of difference between sitting, staying and dropping to command in an empty field or a back garden and doing the same things amidst all the noise, energy and excitement of a shooting day. If the lessons are only superficially absorbed, if the pup still answers commands only when it is ready rather than automatically as a conditioned reflex, then it is not going to sit instantly to the whistle when a cock pheasant has just erupted from cover right under its nose, or crashed to the ground in plain sight 20 yards (18 m) away.

The other main cause of all that careful training breaking down under the pressure of a real day in the field is that the handler allows the dog gradually to take charge of events. Instead of experiencing a sudden rush of blood to the head and taking off into the distance, the young dog slowly pushes back the boundaries of 'acceptable' behaviour. At first it may simply be that you have to repeat the command a couple of times before it sits or comes in to heel. Then it starts to pull farther and farther forward when it is hunting, or is up on its feet ready to go as soon as a bird falls instead of sitting and waiting until you are ready to send it. It all seems quite innocuous: something that you can straighten out at your leisure. But before you know where you are it is running in, chasing rabbits or charging off through the wood and ignoring the whistles. And all that hard work has been ruined.

I should perhaps qualify the term 'ruined' as I am applying it to a shooting dog. The fact that a dog becomes undisciplined, runs in to the fall of game, refuses to answer the whistle, has to be tethered when standing at a drive or kept on a lead instead of staying at heel, does not disqualify it as a shooting dog. There are all too many dogs with some or all of these faults working on shoots; indeed, it would be a rare shoot that didn't have a quota of problem dogs. The fact that the dog runs in or has to be tethered by your peg does not stop you working it. It may still be an excellent game finder and a deadly efficient retriever, or a superb bag filler on the rough shoot. When I say that it has been 'ruined', therefore, it does not imply that it is no longer any use to you on the shoot. What it means is that all the discipline, obedience and handleability that you have spent so much time instilling will be forgotten or ignored. Instead of the part-nership we were aiming for, with the dog working for you, it will start working for itself.

Depending on what type of handler you are, you will then either spend a lot of time and effort trying to keep the dog under some sort of control, pegging it down at every stand or tying its lead to your cartridge belt if you are a walking gun; or you will simply allow it to do as it likes and become progressively more wild. It will still be a working gundog – quite possibly a very good working gundog – but it will not be the dog that it could have become. You will not be able to stand at your peg during each drive, confident

'Keep your dogs in now please.'

that it will sit by your side, marking each bird as it falls but not setting off for a retrieve until you send it. You will not be able to work it on your rough shoot secure in the knowledge that any time it flushes game it will remain sitting or standing still at the point from which it flushed it and not chase along a yard or two behind it. You will not know for sure that you can bring it in to heel with just a couple of peeps on your whistle when it is working in a beating line and the keeper says, 'Keep your dogs in close now please.' In short, a great deal of the pleasure that comes from working a well-trained and well-disciplined gundog will have been lost to you, and in that respect, the dog has been, if not ruined then certainly spoiled.

No matter how hard you have tried to simulate shooting conditions during training – firing shots, bolting rabbits, using dead game for retrieving practice and so on – a real shooting day is immeasurably more exciting for the dog than the best-schemed training session can ever be. Apart from any other considerations your dog will sense your own excitement, and perhaps nervousness, at the prospect of seeing it in real action for the first time. If you are wound up then so will the dog be, and neither of you will react in quite the same way as you would if you were simply carrying out an exercise that you have done a hundred times before.

Moreover, you will no longer be in control of things in the way that you have been during its training. Instead of *you* deciding when to throw a dummy for a seen retrieve, where to hide one for a blind retrieve and when to fire a shot, the real events will happen arbitrarily. That first pheasant will flush when *it* chooses and from where *it* has happened to crouch under the cover of bramble or bracken. If it is shot it will fall where it falls, with no possibility for you to influence the landing site. If it can still run after hitting the ground then run it will. You can no longer orchestrate things to suit your training programme.

You can, however, decide what, and how much, you are going to let your pup attempt to do on its first few outings. You can decide where those first outings will take place. Most importantly of all, you can decide when it has done enough. And when it has, you must stop, no matter how strong the temptation to carry on for just one or two more retrieves, or to let it hunt on for another few minutes. It makes sense to go along to the first few shoots with a definite plan in mind. You could decide that the dog is to be given two or three easy retrieves only, or to walk at heel (or even on the lead) in the beating line on a couple of drives, but no more. It is easier to format a sensible plan for a limited amount of work when you are sitting at home than it is to make such decisions on the hoof, especially when your dog has just done some good work and the temptation is strong to carry on and do a little more and a little more . . .

You will never spoil a young dog by not letting it do enough work during its first few outings. Just a couple of controlled and properly disciplined retrieves will do it far more good than letting it collect a dozen or twenty birds and having it break that discipline and run in on the final one.

The move from training to shooting should not be seen as the end of one phase in the pup's education and the beginning of another, but rather as an extension of your normal training routine. A pup does not graduate from trainee to worker in the manner of a child leaving school one day and starting work the next. It must get there gradually by, in effect, having some 'work experience' brought into its training routine. You do not expect your pup to absorb any of its other lessons in a single session and it would be ridiculous to think that it will be able to learn all the nuances of a proper shooting day on its first introduction. Treat shooting as you have treated all the rest of the training: as something to be picked up a little bit at a time with each lesson properly understood and programmed into the dog's memory before you move on to the next.

The first thing to understand is that you should on no account take your gun with you on these early shooting days. If you want to go shooting then fine, go shooting; but leave the pup at home. You cannot concentrate on your shooting and on your pup at the same time, and any time you are using a gun you had better be concentrating 100 per cent on shooting. A shotgun is a dangerous enough implement when all your attention is on it, and a far worse one if you are trying to shoot with one eye on your dog and one on your quarry. Thus, at the very moment when the pup most needs your undivided attention: as a pheasant rises or a rabbit bolts – you will be fully engaged in handling your gun.

If you are reluctant to lose a shooting day on your own shoot then look around for a neighbouring shoot that will allow you to come along with your pup when they are shooting. Make it plain from the outset that you want to bring your pup along in order to introduce it to shooting. Do not ask if you can bring it to pick up, or worse, to join the beating line, as though it were a fully trained and qualified dog. You do not want to arrive to find that the keeper is relying on you to do a full day's work. Your role is that of a supernumerary. You are there on this day solely to train your dog. Any incidental benefits that you may bring to the shoot will be welcome, and you should certainly try to return the favour they have done you in any way you can short of compromising your pup's training.

If you can be useful as a stop, tapping a fence to prevent birds running out of a drive, or as a marker, standing behind the guns and checking the fall of any wounded birds, then do so by all means. In either case your pup can come along and sit by your side while you are doing your work. Alternatively, once you have completed the 'work experience' programme for the day, you can put the pup away in your vehicle and perhaps offer to join the beaters or act as a flag man, keeping birds from breaking out on the flanks of a drive. An extra pair of hands will rarely be wasted on any shoot, and by returning the favour you have received by being allowed to bring your pup along you increase the chances that any future requests will also meet with a positive response.

If it is possible to arrange something other than a big driven day on a low-ground shoot as your pup's first introduction to the shooting field you should take the opportunity. You are aiming at

The first day out shooting for this young Labrador . . .

. . . and a successful first retrieve.

a gradual transition from training to work and a driven day does not always afford you that luxury. There will be lots of other dogs milling about, and unless you shoot in some very exalted company they will not all be perfectly trained. If there is one thing that is constant in all gundogs it is their ability to pick up bad habits from others. They will not learn to drop to shot, or to sit tightly while pheasants are falling all around them by watching a well-trained dog doing these things, but let them once see another dog run in or chase a hare and they will emulate it with full enthusiasm. Once the first drive gets under way there will be shots ringing out along the line, birds falling on every side, people shouting and whistling at their dogs, and in all likelihood one or two wild dogs flying about the place and clearly having the time of their lives doing exactly those things that you have been so carefully teaching your pup not to do. Unless it is exceptionally calm and collected, even for a Labrador, it is going to wish that it was having a similarly good time – and it may well try to do just that at the first opportunity.

If you have to start your young dog's shooting at a driven pheasant day then I would suggest that at the beginning of the day you leave it in your vehicle until you are ready to start a little light work. Do not bring it out to meet all the other dogs and pick up on their excitement. Try and take it to a spot where it will see only a little bit of the shooting, and concentrate all your attention on it. See how it reacts to the sights and sounds of a shooting day. Is it sitting there calmly watching what happens, or is it gibbering with excitement and looking desperately to get into the action itself? If you think it is totally hyped-up by the experience then try to calm it down. Sit it, talk to it quietly, stroke it and tell it it's a good dog. Do not be tempted to give it a gallop so that it can blow off a bit of steam, nor to try it on a couple of retrieves in the hope that it might settle it. Just let it watch for today. There will be another day later.

Ideally you would not choose a driven day as your pup's introduction to its life's work. Far better to take it out on its own, with a friend to handle the gun for you, and shoot just one or two head for it to retrieve. This is fine if you have access to some ground where you can go along at your leisure and shoot a pheasant or two, a couple of rabbits, some pigeons or maybe a brace of partridge. In reality, most Labrador owners will not be so fortunate. I remember a well-known gundog writer suggesting a cure for a spaniel that was an inveterate rabbit chaser. 'Take it out and shoot forty or fifty rabbits over it, making it retrieve every one' was the gist of the advice, the idea being to sicken the dog of chasing rabbits. It was probably excellent advice – for the man who had the ground, the time, and the ability to go and shoot forty or fifty rabbits in a day. For someone who has no shooting of his own and only works his dog once a fortnight at the invitation of the local syndicate shoot it is impossible.

So whatever advice I or any other writer may give as regards introducing a young dog to the shooting field you have to temper

Do not let your dog race about with the other dogs and get overexcited.

this advice with what is possible and practical in your own situation. The most important thing, though, whether you have every facility you could wish for at your disposal or have to make the best of what little is on offer, is to take your time and bring the pup on slowly. Unless you are training it specifically for finding and flushing game rather than as a retrieving dog you will be well advised to restrict it to retrieving for some time before you allow it to hunt free on a shooting day. You have much more control over your dog when you are sending it out to retrieve a dead bird that you have marked down to a particular spot than when it is hunting free in a situation where live game abounds.

I realise that this is contrary to some of the advice you might read elsewhere, particularly if you are also studying books on spaniel or hunt, point and retrieve dog training. The reason why there is often a greater emphasis on the game-finding aspect of the pup's introduction to shooting is that these breeds are game finders first and retrievers second, and the advice is given on the assumption that the dog is being trained to fulfil its primary function of hunting up game for the gun. You may be training your Labrador with similar priorities, in which case hunting will obviously take precedence over retrieving, but I suspect that most 'general purpose' Labradors will spend far more of their working life retrieving shot birds than they will hunting live ones.

Given the choice, and given that my pup was ready to move on to real work at the start of the grouse season, I would try to introduce it to work on a grouse moor. Starting it on proper work in August would mean that it would have the best part of three months before most low-ground shoots would be in serious action: three months to build on the introduction and work on any aspects of its education that were shown to be in need of extra attention. Ideally, I would try to start it working on a day where the guns were shooting grouse over bird dogs.

Because it would be a dogging day it would be unlikely that more than ten or fifteen brace of grouse would be shot: perhaps a lot less than that on many moors. The dog would be guaranteed a good long walk at heel, with plenty of opportunities for me to keep its enthusiasm in check while the pointing dogs were doing all the real work. We could stand 50 or 100 yards back from the action when there was a point, while the typically open aspect of heather moorland would still allow it to see what was happening. There would not be great volleys of musketry to either scare it or overexcite it – just one or two, perhaps three or four shots at each point, the sound of which would be carried away across the open hill.

There would be other dogs along to retrieve as well as my pup: I would not want it to do any more work than I thought was good for it, nor for it to get the impression that every bird shot was for it to retrieve as of right. If possible I would try to make sure that any birds I sent it for were really dead. I would not want it trying to track a runner just yet, nor attempting to pick a bird that had flown off wounded and then fallen a long way out. The first few retrieves would be as simple as I could make them.

If you can arrange such a day on a grouse moor to start your pup working then seize the opportunity. Do not rush to send it for the first grouse that falls, particularly if there is a possibility that the bird might prove less than a simple, straightforward retrieve. Choose a bird that you are certain (or as certain as you can be) is lying dead in the heather. Walk forward with your dog at heel until you are past the place where the bird dogs are resting, waiting until the grouse have been picked before they are cast off again. Do not send your dog forward from behind where they pointed and allow it to race past them – there is a danger that that might induce unsteadiness in the pointers. Sit it an easy distance downwind from the dead bird and then send it off to fetch it. If it hesitates to pick it up, perhaps puzzled by a new scent, encourage it and when it does return with it make a fuss of your pup – and then put it on the lead. Let the other dogs retrieve the next bird.

Watch how your dog reacts the next time there is a point and more grouse are shot. If it is overexcited steady it down, make it sit and watch calmly while another dog picks the birds. Encourage it to take an interest but be careful not to hype it up. Try to treat this as just one more lesson: putting into practice things the pup has already learned but with freshly shot birds instead of cold game or a dummy. Let it collect a few more birds as the day goes on, but be careful not to overtire it. Walking the hill can be hard work for a young dog, particularly under a hot August sun. If you think it has done enough then stop, and if possible take it home.

It is possible – even probable – that you will not know anyone who might invite you and your pupil along on a day shooting grouse over dogs. Dogging is very much a minority sport and not easy to find, even in those areas where there is heather moorland and a population of grouse. Failing an invite to a dogging day, picking up on a driven grouse day would be my next choice, though I would want to be well back behind the butts, not sitting right beside someone who was killing twenty or thirty birds at each drive. Again, you do not want too much excitement for the pup on its first outing and all that shooting combined with grouse skimming low past the butt and shot birds crashing into the heather could be a little too much for it.

The third option that might present itself for working your dog on the grouse moors is to take him walking up grouse, or working in the beating line on a driven day. Unless it has a very calm character, and unless you are very confident that it will obey you even when grouse are bursting out of the heather under its nose or dropping dead as someone in the line takes a shot, I would strongly recommend that you keep it at your side and on a lead in this situation. A long line such as a flexi-lead would let the dog cover a bit more ground without being beyond your control, though it would also make it a little harder to insist that the pup sit every time a grouse was flushed. If you try running it on a line and find that it is losing discipline shorten the line until you have proper control again.

One problem that is likely to crop up with any sort of grouse shooting is that you may be committed to spending the full day on the hill once you have made a start. The whole team, guns, beaters, loaders, pickers up and flankers, may have to be taken up to the hill in four-wheel-drive vehicles, or even by boat, Argocat or the like. The logistics of a driven grouse day can be frightening, and it may not be practical or possible for you to spend an hour or two on the hill and then leave when you judge that your pup has had enough. And too much work at this stage might be worse for the pup than none at all. If you are picking up you can probably limit your dog's involvement, but if you are walking in line with guns or beaters you may simply have to keep going until the end of the day when the transport comes to take you back off the hill.

Although grouse shooting may offer a number of advantages to the owner who is looking for experience for his new dog it is not something that is available to the majority of Labrador owners. If you live in a part of the country that is far away from heather moorland it may be impossible for you to take the time or find an opportunity to take your pup to a grouse shoot. If this is the case then it will have to make its shooting debut somewhere else.

If you can arrange for your dog's introduction to shooting to take place where there are no distractions from other dogs and guns, then do so. Ideally the only object of the outing would be to give it its first taste of action and matters would be conducted with that in mind, rather than you taking it along to make its debut as an incidental part of the shoot. If you have permission to shoot on some ground with a stock of game and can go along and shoot two or three head at your own convenience, then you can arrange an ideal debut for it.

Your aim is to start bringing together the various aspects of training and letting the dog understand just what its life work will be. This should be a gradual process. Do not decide that you will start it off by taking it to hunt out some rough cover, flush some game, see it shot and then retrieve it. Take one thing at a time.

Unless you are training it primarily as a flushing dog I would suggest that you start it off as a retriever rather than a hunter. You can take your time over a retrieve; a flushed pheasant or a bolted rabbit has to be shot while the chance is there. The choice of what to shoot will obviously depend on the time of the year and the game you have available. From October to the end of January the choice is much wider than during the close season, when you will be limited to pigeons and rabbits or vermin such as crows.

Unless there is no possible alternative do not carry a gun yourself. I make no apology for repeating this: your job is to concentrate on your dog. Get a friend to come along and do the shooting for you. What to shoot depends on what you have on offer: rabbits sitting out on a sunny evening, pigeons flighting into the woods, a walked-up pheasant or partridge, a duck flushed from the flight pond or whatever else is available. The important thing is for you to stay in control of the situation.

If you are walking up keep your dog at heel; if you are standing waiting for pigeons to flight or for a driven bird of some sort then

sit it and make sure that it remains sat. And then await develop-
ments. You may be able to go directly to a field where you know
there will be a multitude of rabbits or a bracken bank where you are
quite certain of raising a pheasant or two, or you may have to sit in
a hide in front of a few decoys and hope that some pigeons will fly
within range. Whatever the situation, sooner or later, if things go
according to plan, there should be some sort of quarry waiting for
your pup to retrieve it.

Impress on your friend with the gun that, having dropped one
bird or bowled over one rabbit, he is not to shoot anything else
until your dog has completed its retrieve. The last thing you want
at this moment is for another shot to be fired and a second bird to
come crashing down just as it is collecting the first one. If you are
confident that there will be other game to retrieve later you could
even elect to make the pup stay and go to collect the first bird or
rabbit yourself, bring it back and let the dog have a good sniff at it.
Alternatively stay with your pup at the sit and ask the gun to go and
collect it. It should not be allowed to develop the idea that every
retrieve is its to collect. Retrieving is something that it does after –
and only after – it has been given the command to fetch.

When you do send it for its first proper retrieve, try to ensure
that it is going to be straightforward. You do not under any circumstances want to start it off with a running cock pheasant or a lightly
wounded rabbit. Nor do you want it to have to swim a river or
negotiate a barbed-wire fence. There will be plenty of time for
those things when it has got a bit of experience. Do not be too
fussed at this moment about the perfect sitting delivery or making
the dog hold the game until you are ready to take it. As long as
it goes out and fetches it and brings it back to you it has made a
good start.

A word of warning at this point. You can add the 'polish' to
your pup's performance as it gains experience. Sitting deliveries
and the like look good and have a certain practical value, but they
can be developed as you progress. Beware though of allowing
serious faults to develop in the early stages and excusing them
with the thought that they too can be ironed out as the dog becomes
more experienced. It is all too easy to ignore unsteadiness or wild-
ness in a young dog with the thought that you can put it right
later. Faults like these can rarely be put right later. Once the dog gets
into the habit of running in you will have the very devil of a job to
stop it. There is a world of difference between getting the dog to sit
before you take the game at the end of a successful retrieve, and
stopping it from bursting away from your side as soon as it sees a
bird fall.

Do not overdo these early lessons – and you should be thinking of them as just that. A few pigeons retrieved during an hour's flighting at dusk is a very different matter to a full day shooting over decoys. If you can manage it, taking your pup out for a short period of 'real' shooting once or twice a week as part of its regular training routine will be far better than taking it for a full shooting day once a fortnight.

It may be that you do not have the luxury of some ground where you can take the pup at your leisure for its introduction to shooting. Indeed, for many gundog handlers working their dogs while others shoot is as much involvement with shooting as they will ever want. In some ways such handlers have an advantage over owners who want to shoot as well as handle a dog, for they can give their full attention to their dogs at all times. If your participation is limited to working the dog on a formal driven shoot you may have no option but to introduce the pup to work during a regular shooting day.

You do not want to be in the thick of the action; most especially, you do not want your dog to be in the beating line, running free in the middle of a dozen or more other dogs. The danger of it being led irrevocably astray is considerable. And even if all the other dogs on the shoot are invariably impeccably behaved you should consider the possibility that your dog might just lead some of *them* astray. Unless working in the beating line is to be its life's work you would do well to keep it right away from the line for the moment.

Try and get yourselves assigned to a relatively quiet spot that will not see much action. How practical this may be will depend a lot on what sort of shoot you attend. If they are planning to shoot over 300 birds during the day there are not going to be many quiet spots to choose from. On the other hand, you may work your dogs on a shoot where a bag of thirty birds for the day is closer to the average, and quiet spots will be freely available. If a big bag is expected you will probably be best to attach yourself to one of the other pickers up who is willing to leave a couple of straightforward retrieves for you while handling the bulk of the day's work with his own dog.

If you know your way around the shoot you may be able to work a drive in arrears as it were, staying behind to collect the odd bird or two after the main shooting party has moved off to the next drive. This will allow you to take your time and settle the dog down with no distractions from other handlers, and no risk that someone else's dog will nip in and steal a bird from under the pup's nose – hardly calculated to improve its steadiness.

A quiet spot well away from the main activity is ideal for introducing your dog to driven shooting.

Be wary of asking your dog to do too much during these early stages. It is all too easy to get carried away, particularly if it is working well. It is far, far better to do a little bit and then stop while things are going to plan than to keep going until things start to go wrong. The idea for these early days is to introduce it to shooting, not to work it into the ground. The more it does the more likely it is that at some point it will get overexcited and start to forget its training.

As well as gradually increasing the amount of retrieving it is allowed to tackle you will also be introducing it to some of the more advanced aspects of its trade. From simple retrieves of dead birds from close at hand it must learn to work further away from you, to track runners and to retrieve wounded game as well as birds that have been killed outright. It will have to hunt cover for birds that fell into a general area rather than go for a single bird that you have marked to a particular place. Note that I say 'you' have marked. In these early stages you should be wary of the information that you receive from the guns as to what has fallen and where.

A grouse moor may be the best place to start your Labrador on real work.

It obviously makes life a lot easier for the picker up when a gun can pinpoint the precise spot where a bird has fallen – provided that the information is accurate. Ideally every gun would know exactly where every bird he shot had dropped and would pass on that information to the pickers up at the end of every drive. In practice such accuracy is almost impossible to achieve, however hard the gun might try. During a busy drive the gun will be trying simultaneously to watch the bird he has just killed, reload his gun and pick the one he is going to shoot next. He may have shot one bird, registered it falling and then switched his aim to another and not seen where the first one fell. In some circumstances, such as when they are placed in a woodland ride, the guns may not be able to see the actual fall of the birds they shoot. Some birds will be wounded but not killed outright and these may fly on for a considerable distance before falling or landing. And some guns, caught up in the excitement of the drive may not remember where their birds fell, or even how many they shot.

It is an unfortunate fact of shooting life that not all guns take as much care as they should when it comes to marking the birds they shoot. Indeed, there are some who seem to lose all interest in the proceedings as soon as they have pulled the trigger and registered either a hit or a miss. Others may be vague about what they have shot, as regards both position and numbers. 'Three or possibly

A grouse brought to hand.

five to pick, somewhere over towards the big wood' is not the ideal set of instructions to receive at the end of a drive, but it is far from uncommon. And we are all familiar with the gun who consistently overestimates his own prowess and claims birds as 'hard hit and probably stone dead' when he actually missed them cleanly.

At the end of a drive, therefore, the pickers up will generally have to conduct a general search of the area around the guns as well as collecting the birds that have been marked down. The dogs will have to hunt on their own initiative rather than being handled out to the fall, or collect birds that they have marked down themselves. This is excellent 'A' Level work for your pupil, but not something to attempt on its first couple of outings. There is too much chance that it will encounter live game or wounded birds, or be tempted to switch birds in mid-retrieve. However, as its experience grows this type of picking up after a drive can be useful as an introduction to the concept of free hunting.

You may be wondering when to introduce it to the beating line, or to start hunting out game on a walked-up shoot. I once asked the handler of a field trial Labrador whether she allowed it to work as a beater as well as a picker up. The look of horror that I received was more than sufficient answer. 'Not until he's finished running in trials' was the actual answer. If someone who has trained a dog to field trial standard – and for retrievers, that is an extremely high standard – is unwilling to work it as a beater for

A day on the hill may require transport like this Argocat to get you there.

fear that it will forget its manners, then you can work out for yourself that the risks posed to good discipline by free hunting are
considerable.

A dog hunting free, out of your sight in thick cover and accom-
panied by a dozen or more other dogs, is exposed to all sorts of
temptations. You are no longer in control of the situation. If it
decides to ignore your whistles, to put its head down on the line
of a running pheasant and bore off through the covert, to chase a
rabbit or a roe deer or cause any other kind of mayhem, it can
do it – and you cannot stop it. Certainly you can punish it afterwards, but it is extremely difficult at times to have any clear idea
of what is happening in the middle of a clump of rhododendrons
or a tangle of brambles, much less to spot a potential problem as
it arises and try and control your dog before any damage is done.

You may feel that I am making too much of the difficulties that
can arise when you work your dog in the beating line. A great deal
will depend on its temperament. Some dogs will take to free
hunting with very few problems, listening to and obeying their
whistles and staying within a sensible distance of their handlers
right from the start. Others will lose their heads completely and
forget everything they have been taught as the excitement builds
up within them. By the time you are ready to introduce your pup
to a beating line you should have a very good idea of how it is likely

When you first take your pup out shooting it is best to leave your gun at home.

to react. Even so, however calm and controlled it may have appeared up until now, you need to take every precaution to ensure that it stays that way.

There is no fixed amount of time or experience after which your pup will be ready to start free hunting. You have to judge the moment for yourself. Unless there is some strong reason for you to bring it into the beating line – perhaps because your shoot is the 'walk and stand' sort where the guns are also the beaters on alternate drives – I would suggest that you leave this aspect of its work until its second season. In fact, I will go further, and say that unless you intend to use it as beating dog you might well be better to stick to picking up and keep it out of the beating line altogether.

The amount of flexibility you have in these matters will depend on the type of shoot on which you work your dog. A big commercial shoot may have a team of a dozen or more people who are employed specifically as pickers up under the guidance of a head picker up, plus a completely separate crew of beaters organised by the keeper. A smaller, more informal shoot may require everyone and every dog to be prepared to tackle whatever job is necessary, perhaps all beating on one drive and split between beaters and pickers up on another.

The introduction to the beating line should be treated like any other aspect of your dog's training and progressed gradually. If you have the facilities to take it out on its own and allow it to hunt out and flush game with no distractions from other dogs, other handlers' whistles, distant gunshots and the like, then so much the better. It is far easier to keep control of your dog when there is only it to watch than when it is mixed in with several other similar-looking dogs. If you have your own ground and can take it out to work on live game during a training session, whether or not you actually shoot any birds, you can 'manage' its introduction to free hunting far better than if you have to do it during an organised shooting day. If you do not have your own ground you can try and find a friendly keeper who will allow you access to somewhere on his shoot, though few keepers are willing to have their coverts disturbed more than is absolutely necessary during the shooting season.

Start the dog off slowly by keeping it at heel while you are beating. The most common problem for handlers of retrievers working as beating dogs is that the dogs hunt too far ahead of the line. Labradors seem to be particularly prone to this because of their natural instinct to put their noses down on the line of a pheasant which has run forward and track it right through the covert. You will rarely attract the ire of the keeper for having your dog working too close to you, but the dog which bores off right through the wood is never popular, even if it does no real harm. If it gets in among several hundred pheasants and flushes them all at once then both of you are going to be seriously un-popular.

So take things very gently at first and be ready to put your dog on a lead if it seems to be getting too excited. Remember that there may be other people signalling to their dogs on whistles identical to yours. You can imagine how confusing that must be for a young dog that has previously only heard one whistle – your whistle – at any one time. Do not assume that it has to be started off working from the very beginning of every drive, nor be allowed to work on right to the end. Better to keep it at heel or on the lead and allow it to get used to the idea before you let it run free. Look for a situation

Introduce it to the beating line very carefully and ensure that you stay in control.

where it cannot get into too much trouble in order to gradually introduce it to hunting in the beating line. The chance may arise near the end of the drive when most or all of the birds have been flushed and there are only a few yards left to hunt out. Alternatively, there may be a relatively open section of the covert where you can allow it a little licence but still be able to keep a close eye on it and stop it if you think there is any sign of it getting away from you.

Send it on to hunt, but try to ensure that it realises that it is still acting under orders: call it back in to you once it has covered a few yards, or make it sit and turn, but do not just let it race off entirely on its own initiative. You need to establish in its mind, right from the beginning, that even though it is off and running among all these exciting scents, it is still working to orders. As it gains experience so it can be allowed to work more on its own initiative. The aim is not to turn it into some sort of robot that mindlessly follows instructions regardless of what its nose is telling it. The reason you are using a dog in the first place is because, using its nose, it can find game that you could not. It will, though, have time to develop those skills after it has learned to harness its enthusiasm and stay within a reasonable distance while hunting.

If all goes well you can gradually allow it to do a little more: perhaps on the next drive, perhaps on the next shoot day. Always try to keep on top of it during these early stages. Turn it and recall it, bring it in to heel for a few minutes, make it sit beside you when the line is halted for any reason. Above all do not let it get the idea that once it is cast off as a member of the beating line it can do whatever it pleases. That idea, if it once takes hold, will quickly be carried over into other aspects of its work.

Be especially wary when letting your dog hunt free for the first time in a field of sugar beet, turnips or the like. Some otherwise steady dogs seem to lose their heads entirely in this kind of cover. It may be because the crashing sound they make when running through the leaves deafens them to their whistles, or it may be something to do with the way that pheasants and partridges run down the drills. Whatever the cause, the effect can be startling, particularly when a previously steady or even staid dog turns temporarily into a galloping nutcase.

Different dogs have vastly differing temperaments: even litter brothers and sisters can be poles apart in the way they react. Your pup may take hunting in its stride and stay properly in hand from the beginning, or it may be one of those which loses its head entirely as soon as it gets a bit of freedom. Obviously, the one needs a different approach from the other. Free hunting is a major test of the basic discipline that the dog should have absorbed during its early training. If it starts to get out of control now the remedy is to stop and go back to basics again. The more it gets away from you now the harder it will be to bring it back into line later.

The start of work is not the end of training. In some ways 'training' of both dog and handler will continue as long as both go out to work in the shooting field. The handler must learn to 'read' his dog: to know from the dog's body language when there is game close to hand and whether that game is furred or feathered, when a wounded bird has run and even when a seemingly missed bird has actually been pricked. The dog in turn will be gaining experience of working with real game: learning to track a wounded bird while ignoring birds which have not been shot, learning that an old cock pheasant has spurs that can inflict a painful scratch if he is not picked up properly.

The ability to read a dog takes time, if only because you cannot

Patience and experience will turn a novice into an accomplished working dog.

know how a dog will react in any situation until after that situation has occurred. Individual Labradors can develop various idiosyncrasies, some of which may even be useful. Pointing birds that are tucked tightly into cover is not uncommon and may well be followed by a pounce resulting in a pegged bird. I once saw a keeper's dog pointing quite staunchly during a walked-up pheasant day. When I mentioned it he chuckled and told me that any bird his dog pointed had better get into the air pretty smartly. 'When she does that,' he said, 'it usually means fly or die.'

A certain bustling and busyness in the dog's attitude will usually mean that there is game – or at least, the scent of game – somewhere close by – a very useful indicator if you are walking up in an area where birds are thin on the ground. You will have to discover what it means when the dog affords cover a cursory glance but makes no attempt to enter it. It may be that the dog's nose has already told it there are no birds to be found in that particular bramble patch, or it could just be that it has decided that it is all too thick and prickly for it to go forcing its way through on the off-chance. Some Labradors love bashing through cover; others see it as a slightly distasteful chore.

The best dogs and the best handlers can develop the sort of partnership where both seem to know instinctively what the other is doing: but such apparently effortless co-operation will usually only arise as a result of an awful lot of hard work. Proper training lays the foundations: a careful introduction to the shooting field builds on those foundations. In the end, though, there is no substitute for experience in turning a raw novice into an accomplished and capable gundog.

6

The Working Labrador

Going shooting feels quite wrong, without a dog to take along,
'Cos half the fun at any shoot, is trying to control the brute . . .
David Hudson

U ntil now any reference to 'work' for our pup has been
roughly divided between picking up and beating. Indeed,
the whole gamut of gundog work can be split into two
categories: finding game for the guns to shoot and collecting it
once it has been shot. Some breeds specialise in finding, others in
fetching, though all are capable of carrying out either function. It
must be said, though, that some are more capable than others.
Training an Irish setter as a non-slip retriever would not be impossible, but it would be challenging, and I question whether
either the dog or the owner would be particularly happy with the
result. Fortunately the Labrador, though bred originally as a
'fetcher', can double as a 'finder' and make a pretty good job of it
into the bargain.

However, although it is convenient to divide dog work into just
two categories, in practice 'finding and fetching' can cover an
extremely broad spectrum. Even a single activity, such as working
in the beating line on a driven pheasant shoot, can differ wildly
between one shoot and another.

Imagine a drive involving 4 acres (1.5 ha) of game crop packed
with six or seven hundred pheasants that are to be gently induced
to take to the wing in threes and fours by a line of beaters, all with
their dogs strictly under control and working close by their feet.
Contrast that with a 40 acre (15 ha) softwood plantation which just
might hold half a dozen birds on a good day, birds which will tuck
themselves tightly under heaps of brashings or run like hares in
preference to using their wings. And imagine that there are only five
or six beaters plus their dogs to cover the whole of the big wood.
'Strictly under control' might still be a good option, but 'close by
your feet' certainly would not.

A dog running wild in the game crop would probably ruin the

Picking up on a grouse moor is an ideal way to introduce your pup to retrieving freshly shot game.

whole drive by sending a big cloud of pheasants forward in a single flush. The same dog let loose in the plantation would probably be considered to have done a good job if, in the course of running wild, it got two or three of those half dozen birds up and over the guns. Not, let it be said, that I am in favour of dogs running wild. I get annoyed with my own dogs every time they do it, which does not necessarily stop them from doing it again.

The sort of work that will be required from your pup when it is ready to take to the shooting field for real can vary enormously according to where and when you are going shooting. As far as this chapter is concerned 'going shooting' includes everyone involved on a shooting day, not just those who are carrying the guns. We will have a look at some of the various types of shooting that you might be involved in, and at the different demands that each will make on your Labrador.

Grouse

The grouse seems a suitable candidate to begin with, if only because 12 August signals the start of a new shooting season for those guns lucky enough to have some kind of access to the moors. A grouse moor is also an excellent place to introduce a young dog to 'real' work. For a start, on a typically bare heather hill you can see where your dog is and what it is doing, and it can see you. There is less inducement to riot than when it is in the close confines of a covert with other dogs racing about, pheasants running, sticks tapping, beaters yelling (yes, I know they should not be yelling, but we are talking about shooting in practice here, not shooting in theory), guns firing close at hand and enough cover so that it can neither see you nor be seen by you most of the time. Life on a grouse moor is generally a little more serene.

There are three ways to shoot grouse: you can drive them, walk them up, or shoot them over pointing dogs. Driven and walked-up grouse offer the two regular sorts of employment for the working Labrador – getting birds on the wing and collecting them after they have been shot – whereas shooting over pointers means that you will only be required for retrieving duties.

If you plan to volunteer your services as a beater on a grouse moor you and your dog should both be reasonably fit. The amount of ground that is brought in on some drives has to be seen to be believed. Not only will you have to cover a lot of ground but you will have to be prepared for it to be both rough and steep in places. And if it rains there is rarely anywhere to shelter. On the plus side you get to see some beautiful country and the exercise is good for you and your dog.

The beating line on a grouse moor will stretch over a wide front – it could be the better part of a mile – and will generally be quite widely spaced. Grouse keepers rarely have as many beaters as they would like. Some quite complicated manoeuvres may be required – bringing both ends of the line round in a flanking movement while the centre marks time, or wheeling the whole line through 180 degrees – and there are obvious difficulties of communication with such a spread-out operation. Beaters are generally equipped with a flag attached to a stick which they flap vigorously as they walk in order to flush the grouse and to send them in the direction of the butts where the guns will be waiting.

The dog's task is similarly to find grouse and flush them. A grouse moor can look like so much bare ground, particularly where the heather has recently been burned, but that apparently bare ground can hold a surprising variety and amount of life. There will be grouse of course and probably mountain hares as well as larks, pipits, curlews, snipe, and a whole range of other birds, mammals and reptiles. It takes very little heather to provide enough cover to conceal a covey of grouse completely, and particularly at the start of the season they can sit so tightly that you practically have to stand on them before they will take to the air. If you are separated

The wide-open nature of the moor makes it easy to keep an eye on your dog as it works.

from your neighbouring beaters by 40 or 50 yards (37 or 46 m) on either side it is quite easy to walk right past a covey and never suspect that it was there.

It is almost impossible to see a grouse when it is tucked down in the heather. On the open spaces of the moor it is only their near perfect camouflage that protects them from predators like the eagle, peregrine and hen harrier. If their nerve holds, if they keep their heads down and if they are not unlucky enough to be sitting directly in your line of march, there is no way that you will spot them. Fortunately they cannot hide their scent from a questing dog, and on days when the birds are sitting tightly dogs are essential to find them and get them on the wing.

A beater's dog can range quite widely on a moor, depending to a large extent on how well spaced the line is. Ideally it should hunt out the heather on either side of the handler and not pull too far forward from the line in case it sends birds back over the beaters' heads. If it is doing its job properly it is going to cover a great deal of ground in the course of the day, so if you are going grouse driving you should make sure that the dog is up to the work as well as being fit enough yourself. A long day beating under a baking August sun can exhaust the fittest of dogs.

If you do not know the moor it is worth enquiring whether there is any water available for the dogs – and doing so before you start out for the first drive. A shortage of water is not usually a problem on a grouse moor – often exactly the opposite, with an excess of the stuff falling on you from the sky. Most hill ground has burns and springs as well as boggy pools where the dogs can drink and wallow, but there are moors where water is in short supply which means that, on a hot day, you will have to carry some with you for when your dog needs it. A bottle in a game bag or one of the ex-army canteens that you can attach to your belt should suffice, but it will be of no use if you only discover the need for it once you are a couple of miles away from where it is sitting in your vehicle.

Keep your eye on the coveys when they fly, as they will often pitch in short of the butts and may have to be flushed again when you reach them. You will not necessarily find them just where you saw them land, since grouse can make good use of their legs and run surprisingly quickly.

As the line of beaters approaches the butts there is usually some kind of signal to tell the guns not to fire any more shots forward – i.e. towards the beating line – and then a second signal to end the drive. You are well advised to keep a sharp eye on what is happening in the butts ahead of you if grouse flush in the last couple of hundred yards of the drive, and be prepared to take evasive action if need be. In theory nobody should ever fire a dangerous shot, but in practice the excitement of driven grouse shooting combined with the fact that they tend to fly low, skimming across the heather, can cause even the best of guns to make a mistake.

It is worth checking in advance whether the beaters' dogs are expected to help with the picking up. This can be quite a contentious issue with some guns, who understandably want their own dogs to retrieve the game they shoot. Because of the ground-skimming flight of grouse it is not advisable to send a dog to retrieve until the drive is over. By the end of the drive a gun may have grouse scattered in the heather all the way round his butt, and hopefully should have a good idea of how many there are to pick and roughly where they fell. The gun may be looking forward to working his own dog on those birds, and the sight of the beater's dogs sweeping up to the butts and hoovering up everything in their path can induce near apoplexy.

Equally, there are guns who lose all interest once the signal comes

When going in to a point ensure that your dog stays back behind the pointing dog.

to end the drive and neither know nor care how many birds are down nor where they fell. Fortunately the majority of guns fall into neither category. Check before you start the first drive what the situation is as regards collecting shot birds and, if asked specifically not to retrieve, bring your dog in to heel or put it on a lead just before you reach the butts. In general, though, all the help that is available is likely to be needed to clear up the game at the end of the drive. Grouse can be surprisingly difficult to find. Before getting too involved in picking up make sure that you are not supposed to be elsewhere. It is quite likely that the keeper may need to get the beaters away quickly from the end of one drive and into position to begin the next one.

Watch your dog and note where it picks each bird. If the gun has taken the trouble to remember where they fell he is unlikely to be impressed if you cannot tell him which of his birds you have picked. Do not be over eager to demonstrate your dog's ability. If one of the other dog handlers is searching for a particular bird it is polite to wait to be asked before sending your dog in to 'help' him. Too many dogs all hunting the same bit of ground can foil the scent and make the job even more difficult.

Picking up on a grouse drive, keeping a low profile close to the line of guns.

Birds that have been hit but have carried on for some distance behind the butt before dropping may have to be left until later if that ground is to be brought in as part of another drive. Check with someone who knows before sending your dog after the bird that is 'lying stone dead beside that grey rock about two hundred yards back'. You will not be popular if you flush a covey or two that should have been left undisturbed until they were sent over the butts. Besides, there may be pickers up employed especially for birds like those, and your dog has almost certainly earned a rest before you start off again for the next drive.

Picking up on a driven grouse day will require a reasonable level of fitness from both handler and dog, though it seldom involves covering anything like the ground taken in by the beating line. There are two places for a picker up on a driven grouse moor: either right by a butt or a long way behind it. Grouse fly low and fast and guns shoot both in front of and behind their butts. If you are told to take up a position behind the butts, find yourself either a peat hag or a gully where you are completely out of sight (and therefore out of shot) of all the guns, or get well back beyond the distance at which a stray shot can cause any damage.

You may be asked to share a butt with a gun who has no dog of his own and collect the birds that he kills. As we have already seen, some guns will have their own dogs and will neither require nor appreciate your services, but you will obviously not be assigned to pick up for one of them. It is up to you to make sure that you do not get in the way of the gun (or of the loader if it is a double-gun day) and you may find this means that you are better to stay just outside the butt. If so, stay *close* to it. 'Your' gun may know where you are but the guns in the neighbouring butts may not, and when concentrating fully on a covey of grouse they might well fail to spot you sitting in the heather. And remember to keep the dog with you until the drive is over. If you send it to collect a shot bird and another covey skims through while it is out there is a strong chance of it being in the way. If the guns see it you will have spoiled their chance of a shot at that particular covey: if they do not you may have a dead or wounded dog on your hands.

Try and remember where every bird that your gun kills has dropped. Some people use a pencil and paper with the butt as the nominal centre of the page to mark each bird and its approximate distance out from the butt. When the drive ends collect (or try to collect) all the birds belonging to your gun before offering your services elsewhere. Do not forget that grouse can run, and the bird that crumples spectacularly and crashes to the ground seemingly dead may just have a broken wing. If it is not where you expected and your dog seems to think it has a line to hunt then let it follow it. It is the one with the nose, not you.

Many keepers prefer their pickers up to be well back behind the line to collect those pricked birds that may carry on for some distance before collapsing. This applies to all forms of driven shooting, not just to grouse. If you can see the butts from where you are standing watch carefully for birds that flinch, twist in their flight, or shed feathers when a shot is fired, but keep on coming anyway. You can often tell by the bird's flight when it has been hit, or by the way that it lands in the heather. Some birds will fly on apparently unscathed and then simply die in mid-flight to thump down into the heather. Others 'tower' when shot, climbing higher and higher and then usually dropping down stone dead.

If you are far enough back to be sure there is no risk to the dog you can send it before the drive is over to collect birds which you are sure can be picked. Once the drive ends collect any others that you have marked and then make your way to the butts to help with the collection of those that dropped closer in. The guns will appreciate being told what you have picked behind them – particularly if you have picked a bird that they thought they had missed – and you should liaise with the other pickers up to ensure that someone does not waste time looking for a wounded bird that is already in your game bag.

Walking up grouse combines the work of the beating team with that of the pickers up. A line of guns, sometimes interspersed with beaters, walks the hill and shoots the grouse as they are flushed. If you are hunting your dog in the line it is important to keep it well in: a grouse rising at 35 yards (32 m) is likely to be out of range before any of the guns can react, and the birds may well rise several yards ahead of the dog. It also needs to be reliably steady since chasing a grouse that is flying just above the heather may be tempting for it but it is extremely annoying for the guns who may be unable to take a shot for fear of hitting the dog. It could also end up being shot by accident by a gun who simply failed to see it. If you are unsure of your dog's steadiness you may be best advised to keep it at heel or on a long lead.

When birds are dropped the line should stop and wait until they have been picked. Do not be tempted to nip back to collect a bird that drops behind the line while the rest of the team march on. The next covey may burst back through the line and put you and your dog in danger. Given the distances covered on a walking-up day the chances are that most of your companions will be only too pleased to take a breather while a bird is being picked.

Beware of being the only one in your part of the line who is carrying a game bag unless you fancy the prospect of carting all the game over your shoulder. Even two or three brace of grouse can become quite a burden after a mile or two walked and a few thousand feet climbed. There is generally a rule that he who shoots a hare carries that hare, and I would advise you to abide strictly by it – unless you shoot the hare yourself and can find some other willing idiot to lug it along for you.

Walking up grouse is often, and quite wrongly, confused with dogging. In practice there are considerable differences. For a start you should not walk in line when shooting over bird dogs. There will be a team of pointers or setters whose job it is to find the grouse. These dogs will quarter the hill under the eye of their handler while the rest of the dogging party walks along in a bunch and watches them work. When a covey is found the dogs will point and two guns will walk forward with the dog handler for the birds to be flushed and shot. Only then will there be a requirement for your Labrador to come and retrieve while the bird dogs take a break.

A grouse carried to hand.

Picking up on a grouse moor for a dogging party can be an excellent introduction to real work for a young Labrador. The pace of the day is generally fairly relaxed and the action sporadic. You will have ample warning of when shots will be fired and there will usually be only one or two birds to collect after each point. There may be more if the guns are on good form but equally there may be none. The sort of frantic action that can occur around the butts during a busy drive never happens when dogging, nor is there the temptation to chase caused by coveys flushing right under a young dog's nose, as can happen in the beating line. You will usually be a reasonable distance away from the guns when birds rise, and on the open hill the sound of the shots is quickly dispersed.

There are a few rules to remember. It is a great help to the bird dogs if the party stays together and avoids the temptation to spread out across the hill. It is also far more sociable and allows you to talk – quietly – to your companions while the setters or pointers are finding some grouse for you. Those setters or pointers, and their handler, will not appreciate any help that your Labrador might decide to offer in the matter of finding birds. Until there are birds to be picked it should be kept at heel or on a lead.

In particular, never allow it to get ahead of a dog which is on point. If you are taking part as a gun as well as working your dog, sit it and tell it to stay when you go forward to a point or, better still, slip a lead round its neck and ask another member of the party to hold it. That way you can concentrate on your shooting without having to worry about what your dog is up to. And do not send it to retrieve as soon as the first bird hits the heather; wait until the bird dogs have lifted all the grouse from the covey and been collected up by their handler and the guns have unloaded. Then, and only then, is it time to start picking up the shot birds.

Retrieving a grouse that you have seen drop into short heather 30 yards (27 m) ahead of you looks easy for the dog, and most of the time it really is as easy as it looks – but not all the time. Sometimes an apparently 'easy' retrieve can baffle every dog in the party. This is particularly so when a bird drops into long heather, or down in a peat hag where it is sheltered from the breeze which would carry its scent to the dogs. Frustrating as this can seem it can also be excellent training for both handler and dog, demonstrating the vagaries of scent and the need for persistence when a bird has been seen to drop.

Driven Shoots

Driven shooting, with the obvious exception of driven grouse, usually takes place on low ground, though some moorland shoots release partridge on ground where grouse are no longer a viable proposition. The term covers an enormous range of sport, from wild bird shoots where no birds are released and a bag of twenty or thirty would be considered a good day, right up to the big commercial ventures where a let day could result in a bag numbered in the high hundreds. On a grouse moor the beating line can stretch over miles of open country simply because the grouse are truly wild and the beaters must go to the birds. On a low-ground shoot careful management by the keeper will normally see the birds concentrated in woods or game crops specifically designed to ease the task of presenting them over the guns.

The amount of planning and organisation that goes into a driven shoot will vary as much as the size of the bag. One shoot may require nothing more than that the guns stand at one end of the wood while the beaters go in at the other end and turn their dogs loose. Another may employ stops to prevent the birds running through the drive, flankers to stop them flying out at the sides, ropes of sewelling to persuade them to flush at the right place and separate teams of beaters to blank in outlying parts of the covert. As I have said, there may be hundreds of birds in the covert or there may be just one or two. Although all driven shoots are similar in theory they vary enormously in practice. Dog work of a standard that is gratefully received on one shoot might ruin the day completely on another.

In an ideal world every keeper would make certain that all the beaters, stops and pickers up knew exactly what was expected of them on each drive, and indeed there are many keepers who are experts in getting their team to do just what they require. Sadly, there are others who assume that everybody knows instinctively what is wanted and as often as not blow their lids when someone does not follow to the letter the instructions that they have not actually been given.

You can help the keeper and yourself by always trying to be clear about what is expected of you. If you are not sure go and ask. As a general rule, though, in any beating line it is better to have your dog too close to you than to let it get too far out. It has to be said at this point that your dog is unlikely to agree with that statement. Look at it from the dog's perspective. It is in a wood which will be positively reeking with the fresh scent of game birds. There are pheasants running through the bushes in plain sight just ahead of it, there are lots of other dogs bustling about, there are handlers whistling and shouting commands to those dogs, sticks tapping, guns firing and birds rising with a clatter of wings. It must be tremendously exciting, particularly for a young dog, and the temptation to rush off and do its own thing will be enormous.

Sadly, the greater the temptation the more important it is that your dog does not give in to it. If there are only a few birds in the wood there may be no harm done if a dog charges through to the end of the drive and flushes them. If there are thousands, and the drive is intended to provide steady shooting for the better part of an hour for eight paying guns, the same behaviour could spell disaster. We considered the best time to introduce a young dog to the beating line in chapter 5, but it is certainly not at a big commercial shoot on a thousand-bird let day.

The role of the beating line is to get birds into the air and flying in the direction of the guns. This may mean flushing them wherever they are found, or it may mean moving them quietly through the covert until they concentrate at a flushing point. On some drives your job may be blanking in, that is not flushing game at all but rather getting the birds to run ahead of the beating line and into another covert from which they will eventually be flushed. This can be confusing for your dog, particularly if it is accustomed to working on a rough shoot and being encouraged to press birds until they take wing. Now there are pheasants trotting along in front of it and you are keeping it back. Incidentally, it can be instructive on occasion to get yourself down to the dog's-eye level and have a look

A great deal of planning and organisation goes into a successful driven shooting day.

at what it can see ahead of it. Often what appears to be quite dense cover from 6 ft (2 m) above the ground will have a lot of open space at ground level which means that while you may be seeing just bushes your dog may have a clear view of the birds running through the undergrowth in front of it.

When a lot of birds have run ahead of the line and gathered at the end of the wood, or at the sewelling or wire netting which has been strung across the drive to stop them running and encourage them to get into the air at the flushing point, there is an obvious temptation for a dog to race in and scatter the lot. Unless the keeper specifically asks you do this – and it is possible that he might if, for example, the guns have already shot their quota for that drive – you are unlikely to be popular if your dog gives in to the temptation. Your job is more likely to be to stand, with the dog sitting at heel, or on the lead, and tap with your stick to keep the birds from breaking back through the line. Only when – or if – you are instructed to 'take it on through' should you let your dog press forward to flush those birds which have tucked into cover and elected not to fly with the rest.

Some shoots make a clear distinction between beaters and pickers up; others will take a more flexible approach with roles switching between the two tasks. Much will depend on the number of bodies available. Obviously there have to be beaters working through the cover and flushing the game or there will be no birds to shoot. If there is a shortage of hands then picking up can be left until the drive is over and accomplished with the beaters' or the guns' own dogs. However, pressing all spare hands into the beating line can cause problems, as some handlers are understandably reluctant to use their dogs as beaters, particularly those with youngsters in their first working season. Picking up can be tightly controlled, running in the beating line can approach anarchy. If you are not willing to use your Labrador in the beating line you should make this clear when you first agree to come and help out on a shoot day. It is hardly fair to the keeper if he suddenly finds that of the dozen beaters he thought he had arranged, three or four are only willing to stand behind the guns and pick up.

If you are picking up you will often be asked to stand well back from the line so that you can see as much as possible of what is happening in front of you. Watch particularly for wounded birds: those with a leg down, those that jerk to a shot but then fly or glide on, and those which crash down with a broken wing only to get to their feet and run. Your first priority is to gather the wounded and the birds that fall back behind the line; the dead birds lying out in the open can be collected by the guns themselves or by their dogs. Note what you have picked and check with the guns at the end of the drive to see that, if at all possible, every bird that was shot has been collected.

This checking is obviously easier on a drive where a couple of dozen birds have been killed than one where there are a couple of hundred to pick. Some of the pickers up will often be expected to stay behind and finish collecting the birds from one drive while the guns and the beaters go off to the next. If you are asked to stay behind and are new to the shoot make sure you, or one of your fellow pickers up, know where the next drive will be, and how to get there. Always check that any birds that fall well back can be collected without spoiling another drive. If you are in doubt about whether it is safe to send your dog into a wood to collect a runner, ask first.

If you are picking up at a driven partridge shoot rather more care is needed about selecting your position than at a pheasant drive. In general pheasants that fly low through the line will be left for another day, when hopefully they will present a more sporting shot. Partridges, though, are more akin to grouse in that they may skim the ground, and they will often be considered as sporting birds to be shot if possible, even though they are flying at a height at which a pheasant would almost certainly be ignored. This means that a picker up standing close behind the line could be a considerable

It is always better for your dogs to be too close rather than too far away during a drive.

nuisance to the guns by restricting their safe arc of fire if they have spotted him, and a potential accident victim if they have not. The safest place for the picker up on a partridge shoot, or indeed on a pheasant shoot where some partridges may come through with the pheasants, is either well back and out of shot or actually in the line next to one of the guns.

Rough Shooting

Rough shooting is used to cover an enormous variety of sport, and any definition of the term will hinge, to some extent, on what that individual considers to be a formal day. If you regularly shoot several hundred driven pheasants in the course of a day you might consider the sort of 'beat one drive and stand the next' shooting day that yields forty or fifty birds as a rough shoot. If a forty-bird day is the highlight of your season you might take a different view. For our purposes we will consider a rough shoot to be the sort of day where there are no formal drives; where walked-up birds are shot, possibly with some impromptu driven ones as well, and where the emphasis is on hunting rather more than on marksmanship.

Its very nature makes it almost impossible to generalise about rough shooting. You may find yourself hunting out a hedgerow or wading through a snipe bog; beating through a forestry plantation or walking up a field of sugar beet. You may be bolting rabbits from a gorse bush or creeping up to a pond in the hope of flushing some duck; beating through thick cover in the hope of a woodcock or waiting to ambush pigeons flighting into a wood to roost. Above all else, a rough-shooting Labrador needs to be versatile.

One of the commonest forms of rough shooting is for the guns – perhaps just one or two, or as many as a dozen – to walk in line with their dogs hunting out the cover in front of them and flushing any game that they find. Typically, on such a shoot your dog will have to work a whole range of cover in the course of a day, depending of course on where the shoot is and on what sort of ground. There could be stubbles or grass fields, boggy ground or bracken-covered hillsides, hedgerows and ditches, or any sort of woodland from ancient stands of open hardwood to densely planted conifers, coppiced woodland or naturally regenerated scrub.

Your dog will have to learn to work all of these vastly differing types of cover and more, and to recognise and hunt out every sort of game. Variety is the essence of the rough shoot, and a single day anywhere in the country could see rabbit and hare, pheasant and partridge, snipe and woodcock, pigeon, any of half a dozen kinds of duck and possibly even a goose in the bag. If the rough shoot borders on moorland you might add grouse, blackgame and even capercailzie to that list, not to mention the various kinds of vermin such as crows, jays, magpies, grey squirrels or mink that might cross your path.

Steadiness, particularly steadiness to the flush and fall of game, is – or should be – a vital part of the rough-shooting Labrador's training. It is not uncommon to hear an owner excusing bad behaviour on the part of his dog by saying, 'He's only a rough shooting dog', but in fact, it is just as important, and arguably even more important, for the rough-shooting dog to be steady than one which spends its working life sitting by your side on driven days. If your driven-shooting dog is unsteady, you can put a lead round its neck and fasten the other end to some sort of tether. No such 'cure' is available for the rough shooter. His dog has to hunt freely in all

Rough shooting can provide a great deal of variety for the working Labrador.

kinds of cover. When a pheasant or a hare is flushed, all his attention, at least momentarily, is going to be concentrated on trying to add it to the bag, not on handling the dog and ensuring that it does not give chase. While chasing something that is flying is a breach of discipline, chasing a hare or a rabbit, particularly if it runs across the line of guns, is potentially far more serious. In thick cover a gun may be able to see the quarry but not the pursuing dog, and the possible consequences are obvious.

Rough shooting does not mean low standards of dog work. If anything the rough-shooting Labrador should work to a higher standard than, for example, one that is used only to pick up on a driven shoot. It has to switch from flushing dog to retrieving dog each time a bird is shot, to work closely enough to its handler to ensure that birds are not flushed out of range, and still hunt keenly enough to find game which is probably pretty thin on the ground. If the handler is also shooting, the dog has to be responsible enough not to require constant handling. It is impossible to concentrate on your dog at the same moment as you are trying to get the gun onto a woodcock jinking through the trees or swinging onto a springing partridge. In short, rough shooting is a wonderful sport, but it is not an easy apprenticeship for your dog before graduating to the more formal atmosphere of driven shooting. If anything the opposite is true.

Wildfowling

The Labrador is the archetypal wildfowler's dog. Its ancestors were bred to work in the cold waters off the Newfoundland coast and with its thick coat and love of the water it is ideally suited for dawn and dusk flights on the frozen wastes of foreshore and estuary. It is generally mentally as well as physically suited as a dog for the wildfowler, willing to sit motionless for hours at a time and endure mornings of cold and wet, often without even a single retrieve to enliven its outing.

Wildfowling is a solitary sport, though sadly it is becoming increasingly difficult to find any sort of solitude around our coasts as more and more wildfowlers try to fit into the areas open to them – areas incidentally, which are continually shrinking as marshes and estuaries are developed or become designated as nature reserves, or as politically motivated local authorities ban wildfowlers from their traditional haunts. A wildfowler's Labrador may be almost as important to its owner as a companion as a working retriever, though there is no question that its retrieving abilities can be tested to the full when there is a goose to retrieve from a fast-flowing gutter or a duck drifting out to sea on the tide.

Wildfowling is a sport that positively thrives on weather that would see many other forms of shooting abandoned. Gales, blizzards and sub-zero temperatures are the very essence of fowling out on the foreshore, and it takes a tough dog to withstand them. To sit motionless out in the wind and snow for hours at a time, particularly if it is soaked from swimming to collect a duck from the tide, puts a considerable strain on even a Labrador's ability to withstand the cold. The old adage that, at the end of a shooting day your priorities should be first your dog, then your gun, and then yourself, is never more true than when applied to the wildfowler. A wet, frozen dog coming off the shore or the marsh needs to be dried, fed and given somewhere warm and comfortable to rest and recover. A handful of damp straw in a draughty kennel is not what is needed and may eventually result in your dog having to be retired early with rheumatism or arthritis.

Inland duck shooting is considerably less arduous than lying out on the foreshore in the mud. A well-fed flight pond can yield excellent sport as the ducks whistle in from the darkening sky to gorge themselves on barley or potatoes. As on the foreshore the dog's role is to sit quietly beside you and wait for the ducks to fly into the ambush. Some dogs become adept at hearing or sensing incoming ducks long before their owners are aware of them, and pricked ears and a sudden alertness from your dog may well indicate that some sort of action is on the way.

Some guns like to collect their ducks as they are shot, sending the dog to retrieve each time a bird is brought down. There is less chance of losing birds in the dark if you do this, though there is also the chance that other birds flighting in to the pond will see the retrieving dog and sheer off. If you are shooting with companions it is essential that you agree in advance how you will handle picking up, and that you let them know when you are sending your dog for a retrieve. More than one dog has been shot by a gun who heard it splashing in the pond and mistook it for a wounded duck.

Picking up at the end of the flight is complicated by the fact that you often cannot tell which of the shot birds has been collected. The dog disappears into the night and then comes back with a duck in its mouth. Meanwhile your companions are also collecting birds with their dogs so that after a few minutes you will have no idea which birds have been picked and which still await collection. Moreover, you may not have a clear idea of exactly how many there are to pick, since in the dark it is all too easy for two of you to shoot at the same bird. If it drops you may both claim it without realising that another gun has also added it to his personal score. Conversely, a bird that you thought you had missed cleanly may crumple and fall after it has disappeared into the night.

Experienced Labradors often become adept at registering which birds have been hit even if there are no signs obvious to the gun. This is a particularly valuable asset when shooting a flight pond after nightfall, and can help to put birds in the bag that would otherwise be left for the foxes, crows and other scavengers.

Pigeon Shooting

Shooting pigeons over decoys or as they flight into the woods in the evenings is somewhat similar to wildfowling or duck flighting as far as the requirements of your dog are concerned. Its principal task is to retrieve shot birds, with the secondary duties of keeping you company and possibly alerting you to incoming birds if it spots them first.

If you are using dead pigeons as your decoys it may take a little while to accustom your dog to retrieving only the shot birds while leaving the decoys in position. It is in this kind of situation that the more advanced training comes into its own, with the ability to handle the dog onto a particular bird being especially useful. Any dog that is regularly used when decoying pigeon should soon get the idea that it is only the freshly killed birds that are required. Leaving the decoys alone can be particularly difficult to get over to a young dog with limited experience on real game.

Remember that all through your dog's training it has been used to collecting dummies which will have been covered in your scent; now you want it to ignore the decoys which you have handled and left your scent on and concentrate on the other birds. It is understandable if its first instinct is to go for the familiar-smelling birds. Do not forget that just because you can see the fall of a bird it does not follow that your dog can as well. It will be sitting or lying in the hide beside you, but it will not be able to peer over the top as you can. If you design your hide so that the dog can see out through a gap at its eye level it will be a considerable help to it when marking down birds.

Deer Stalking

Deer stalking as a sport enjoys a much lower profile than game shooting. A lot of deer stalking, and woodland stalking in particular, tends to take place at dawn and dusk and this means that few casual observers ever see the stalker at work. It would surprise many people to know that there are deer living in the woods and fields close to them, and that dedicated early risers are out there in the small hours hunting them with their rifles.

It might seem that the deer stalker would have little call for the services of a Labrador, but in fact a dog is often a vital link in the process of bringing a deer to the larder. The principal requirement of a deer stalker's dog is to find the carcass of a deer that has been shot, or to track down a wounded beast. It may seem strange to someone who is not a stalker that a dog would be needed to find something the size of a dead deer, but anyone who has experience of woodland stalking will know just how easy it is to lose a beast without a dog to assist.

Shoot a deer through the heart or through the lungs with an expanding bullet that meets the minimum muzzle velocity and muzzle energy requirements of the various Deer Acts and it *will* be dead a few moments after the bullet strikes. However, during those few moments it may well run for anything from a few yards to a hundred yards or more and it will not necessarily run in a straight line. And a combination of recoil and muzzle flash may mean that the rifleman will not have seen which direction it took, nor even be absolutely certain that his shot was accurate. It is possible that the beast will be dead, but there is also a chance that it may have been wounded or even missed completely.

Let us begin by assuming that the shot was on target and the animal is dead.

This means that, having run up to 100 yards or so, its body could be lying anywhere in an area of about 6 acres. If that area is covered with closely packed Sitka spruce or birch scrub the stalker may find it almost impossible to locate it, even given certain clues such as a blood spoor. A good dog, though, can probably take you straight to it.

A far worse situation occurs when you have shot a deer and failed to kill it outright. Then your only hope of finding it again and administering the *coup de grace* may be to have a trained dog available to track it for you. Pumped full of adrenalin, a wounded deer can cover a considerable distance before it eventually lies down and either succumbs to its injuries or struggles to survive despite them. Tracking such a beast for any distance is way beyond the capabilities of the vast majority of stalkers, though well within the remit of an experienced deer dog.

Basic deer work consists simply in taking the dog to the point at which the beast was shot and encouraging it to track it down to where it has fallen. On a reasonably fresh spoor there should be ample scent to guide the dog once you have got it 'switched on' to it. Assuming that the shot was not a clean miss there will normally be blood, hair and possibly fragments of bone scattered about from the exit wound and it should not be difficult to get even a complete novice interested in this.

You may find that running the dog on a long line will be helpful since there is a danger that it too will disappear into the cover, leaving you with the problem of finding the dog as well as the deer. Unfortunately, in the type of situation where a line would be of most use – very dense cover – it is least practical to employ one. Some handlers fix a small bell to the dog's collar and use it to guide them to the dog, and hopefully the deer.

The best way to train your dog to work deer is to contact a local stalker and ask him if he will allow you to let the dog 'find' some carcasses that he has shot. You can set up an artificial situation initially, using a dead beast, or you may be able to take your dog along on an actual stalk, though you will probably have to wait back at your car until after the shot. With experience a good dog can track down a shot beast hours (or even days if the weather has been kind) after it was actually wounded. The British Deer Society maintains a register of dogs that have been trained to track wounded deer and are available to aid local stalkers.

The other aspect of deer work is to use the dog during the actual stalk. A lot of woodland stalking is done from high seats, with the

Two Labradors, father and son, which specialise in deer work with a professional stalker.

stalker sitting quietly in a tree or up a tower above the woodland floor and waiting for the deer to appear. Other stalkers prefer the considerably greater challenge of getting out into the woods and trying to get within range of the deer rather than waiting for deer to come to them. This involves a great deal of creeping about and peering through binoculars, always with the wind coming from the deer to the stalker and with the odds very much in favour of the quarry.

One of the most difficult aspects of woodland stalking is spotting the deer before it can see, hear, wind or sense you. If you have only seen deer in the open spaces of a zoo or a deer park you will find it difficult to appreciate how something the size of a roe or even a fallow can be practically invisible until it suddenly bounds off. A well trained Labrador that will stick closely and quietly at your heel can be a great help in indicating the presence of deer that it has either scented or seen from its lower viewpoint. 'Closely' and 'quietly' are the key words here, and it is vital that the dog understands its task and doesn't get distracted by other scents such as pheasants or rabbits.

There is a wide difference between using your Labrador as an occasional aid to find a dead deer and training it as a proper deer dog. On parts of the Continent deer work is seen as a sport in its own right and there are tests for deer dogs similar to our own field trials for shooting dogs. The best deer dogs can follow a blood trail which is several *days* old, track down and bay or seize a wounded deer or, having found a dead beast, come back to their handlers and lead them to the deer. Training a deer dog is quite specialised work, well described by Guy Wallace in his book *The Versatile Gundog*. That said, if you have shot a deer in the woods and are unable to locate the carcass there is every chance that your Labrador, if taken to a spot just downwind of where you think the beast should be and told to seek, will quickly find it for you.

There is a tremendous variety of work available for the working Labrador. Even if you do not shoot there are still plenty of opportunities to work the dog with those who do, whether as a picker up or a beater or to find deer for a stalker. That work can take you out onto the hill in the heat of summer in pursuit of the red grouse or onto the foreshore in the depths of winter with a grey goose as your quarry. Training and working the dog, though, are only part of the pleasure of owning a Labrador. Millions of households throughout the country keep dogs of every variety simply for the pleasure of their company. The working Labrador takes the concept of a family dog a step further and may actually earn its own keep as well as giving years of pleasure both at work and at home.

7

Buying an Adult Dog

So I joined this shoot, paid a lot of loot, for some healthy, outdoor fun,
Bought a thick tweed suit, green wellie boots and a hand-made English
*   gun,*
Got a four-wheel-drive and some Grand Prix fives, got a leather-bound
*   shooting log,*
Looked a first class toff, so to round things off, I got a trained retrieving
*   dog.*

David Hudson

There are many potential Labrador owners who would prefer to avoid the undeniable hassle of rearing a puppy from eight or nine weeks of age until it is ready to begin training for the field or to take shooting. While there is no denying the appeal of a Labrador puppy there is also no denying that raising it involves a considerable amount of time and effort. House-training time can be fraught, especially if some members of your household do not fully share your enthusiasm for gundogs in general and this gundog in particular. Some family arrangements may not be suitable for introducing a young puppy, perhaps because you have young children or an elderly relative in residence. The demands of earning a living may mean that you are unable to give a puppy the attention it needs, or your home may not lend itself readily to the demands of puppy rearing.

Raising the puppy may not in itself present a problem, but there may still be plenty of other reasons to choose an adult dog instead of a youngster. You may want a dog that you can work straight away – this season or perhaps even this week – rather than a puppy which will not be ready to enter for at least a year and possibly two. You may not have the time or the resources to train a pup from scratch, or you may simply prefer to leave the training to a professional, perhaps because you feel that you lack the ability to take a raw puppy and turn it into a polished worker. Or you may just prefer to buy an older dog.

There are various advantages, and inevitably some disadvantages, in choosing an adult Labrador rather than a puppy. You can

A well-trained Labrador is worth a great deal of money.

make a far better judgement of the temperament of an adult than of a pup, and obviously you can see the dog's conformation rather than trying to assess it from the way his parents were built. There is no danger that it will grow and grow until it has the build of a Rottweiler, nor that it will fail to grow on and end up as a sort of half-sized replica of a Labrador. If you are buying a trained or partly trained dog you can actually see it at work before you commit yourself to the purchase. You do not have to suffer the delights of house training, of preparing four meals a day, of chewed up shoe laces and sharp little teeth nipping at your ankles when it wants to play. You will not be kept awake at night by the howling in the kitchen or the kennel in the yard, and your garden will not be wrecked by a juvenile delinquent Labrador burying things in the flowerbeds and then digging them up again.

A trained dog is a known quantity. You will not spend six months rearing and twelve months training it only to discover somewhere along the way that it is hard-mouthed, gun-shy or terrified of water. It should be past the stage where it might develop hip dysplasia or have problems with its shoulders, its inoculations should all be up to date and it should be well beyond most of the illnesses that can blight a puppy's youth. Taking on a puppy with the aim of turning it into a working gundog involves a great deal of risk; buying a trained dog means that most of those risks can be eliminated.

But as I have said, there are also disadvantages in buying an adult dog. The first and most apparent is that an adult, and particularly a professionally trained adult, is going to cost considerably more than a puppy. Just how much more will depend on the stage in training that the dog has reached – or is claimed to have reached. However, to make a realistic comparison between the cost of buying a puppy and a trained dog it is necessary to look beyond the initial outlay.

If you buy a puppy you will have to bear the cost of its food, toys, collars and leads and veterinary attention from about eight weeks old until it is fully grown and trained. Taken over eighteen months or two years these will add up to a sizeable sum, depending very much on your choice of diet for the pup and whether it has had to visit the vet for anything other than routine matters such as inoculations. Add in the cost of boarding kennels if you would have left it behind while you went on holiday, and perhaps some expenditure on netting and fence posts to make the garden puppy proof, and the extra price of an adult dog may begin to look quite a bargain. And so far we have said nothing about the time spent in training.

There are various alternatives open to you if you would prefer to buy an older dog rather than a puppy. At one end of the spectrum would be a young adult dog that had been given no training for shooting; at the other would be a fully trained and experienced dog with one or two seasons' actual work behind it. In between there is every possible intermediate stage. I once wrote a tongue-in-cheek guide to help the prospective purchaser of a trained dog translate the jargon from advertisers' parlance into everyday English. Here is part of it – not really serious of course, but there is an element of truth somewhere within.

> *Ready to train.* Means 'ready to start training'. So far simple and straightforward, but beware . . .
>
> *Part trained.* Also means 'ready to start training' but in this case the pup will sit, briefly, when you appear with its food bowl.
>
> *Just needs polishing.* Means 'ready to start training' but will sit for his supper and may even come back when it is called – provided it has nothing better to do at the time.
>
> *Perfect rough-shooting dog.* Means 'too wild to be let off in company'.
>
> *Ideal for driven game.* Means 'will pick up dead birds from a grassy field but won't face cover.'
>
> *Fully trained to a high standard.* Means 'be prepared to write a very large cheque'. It also means that you are entitled to expect a very well trained dog, or your money back – provided that you do not ruin it by letting it run wild the first time you take it out.

Rehoming an Adult Labrador

Although a well-trained Labrador will almost inevitably command a premium price, buying an adult dog need not be a particularly expensive option. There can be any number of reasons why an older dog – and in this context I am using 'older' to denote any Labrador of about nine months and upward – might be offered for sale. Some breeders will run pups on well into adulthood from choice; others may have older dogs to sell because they were unable to find homes for them when they were puppies. A commercial dog breeder may want to see every pup sold and away by the time the litter is nine or ten weeks old, but the owner who takes a litter from his working bitch may feel no such pressure to move the pups on.

Some trainers prefer to keep a litter on until the pups are well

Two first-class working Labradors, both trained by their gamekeeper owner.

grown before deciding which they will keep and which they will sell. This is obviously a much more expensive option for the breeder than selling them all off as soon as they are weaned and the price is likely, though not certain, to reflect this. The breeder may be becoming desperate to move the pups on: young Labradors can eat an awful lot of food and take a great deal of time and attention to look after. It is not uncommon to see young adult Labradors advertised at little or no more than the price of a puppy, and this will not automatically mean that there is something inherently wrong with them. As in all deals involving dogs it is a case of *caveat emptor* – 'let the buyer beware'.

There is also the possibility of taking on a dog that is being rehomed. This can happen for all sorts of reasons: the breakdown of a marriage, the arrival of a new baby, a new job forcing a house move or simply the owners finding that the reality of keeping a dog is not for them. Try the advertisements in your local paper, or check with one of the dog rescue centres if you feel that one of these 'unwanted' pets might suit you. Some of the rescue organisations refuse to pass on their charges to working homes, which always strikes me as a rather strange policy, but there are some strange folk around the dog world. If they do not want the dog to go to a working home then go and look somewhere else.

The most important thing from the point of view of the prospective new owner of one of these adult outcasts is to establish, if at all possible, the real reason why it has become surplus to somebody's requirements. There may be excellent reasons for the owners to feel they must part with their pet, but those same factors might be excellent reasons why you should not consider taking it on. The dog may be vicious, neurotic, hyperactive, a stock worrier or a chronic runaway. It may have become that way because its owners did not know how to raise and train it properly, but it may just be an exceptionally awkward brute. In either case your subsequent attempts to turn it into a well-trained gundog are going to be made considerably more difficult by its early experiences.

Equally it may be a model of good behaviour which has to be rehomed through no fault of its own. It is up to you to listen to the reasons why the dog is on offer and then decide whether you believe them or not. Some rescue organisations, like many responsible breeders, insist that any dog they sell which subsequently becomes unwanted should be returned to them for rehoming. This not only shows an admirable sense of responsibility on the part of the organisation, but it also makes it less likely that you will be palmed off with some anti-social brute simply in order to get it off the present owner's hands.

Whatever the background, if you are considering rehoming a dog, be sure to take plenty of time to get to know the dog before reaching a decision.

Buying a Trained Labrador

Buying a trained adult dog is a totally different proposition from rehoming one that has become available through mischance. Trained dogs may occasionally come on the market because their owners have been forced to give up shooting for some reason, but more usually they will be offered for sale having been trained with a sale in view from the beginning. There are any numbers of trainers, both amateur and professional, who rear and train gundogs and then sell them on when their training is completed. A good Labrador that is ready to take shooting can fetch a high enough price to justify the time spent raising and training it. Such trained dogs can come onto the market for a variety of reasons.

Whether trained professionally or by an amateur, a careful first introduction to shooting is vital.

Many professional dog trainers will bring on young dogs as a matter of course with the specific intention of selling them on when their training is completed. Others, who have field trial honours in mind, sometimes sell a young, trained dog because, once its training has been completed, or partly completed, they find that it is unsuitable for competition. This does not necessarily mean that the dog has a serious fault such as whining, a hard mouth or a poor nose, or that it has been impossible to train to a high enough standard to compete. It may be that it simply lacks the sparkle that would impress the judges. There is little point in a trainer who may have several trialling dogs under his care 'wasting' an entry on a dog that he believes will be unlikely to feature in the honours. Such dogs may never make field trial champions but they can still make excellent shooting dogs.

A dog that has genuinely been trained to retriever field trial standards can make an outstanding shooting dog. The reason why the trainer has decided to sell it is clearly important, even if it does not impinge on its ability as a shooting dog. It may be too soft or too headstrong to suit the trainer. The latter may simply have better dogs in his kennel and not enough time to devote to them all, or the dog may indeed have some fault that would prevent it winning a trial. In any case, the trainer should be willing to give you full details of his reasons for selling the dog. If you are doubtful, or suspect that you are not being told the whole truth, be very careful about parting with any large sums of money.

'Trained' dogs, as we saw earlier, may be offered for sale at almost any stage in their training, from youngsters that have just been taught basic obedience right up to adults with several seasons' shooting behind them. In general, the more experienced the dog the higher the price tag is likely to be – up to a point. A three- or four-year-old with one or two full season's work behind it would probably command a premium price. From five years old onwards, although the dog's experience may be even greater, the price will begin to reflect the number of years that the dog is likely to continue working, and will start to fall accordingly.

Whatever stage in its training the dog may have reached it is important – vital even – that buyer and seller both understand precisely what it has learned and what practical experience it has been given. And when the seller is telling you what the dog has done make sure that any technical terms he uses mean the same thing to you as they do to him. I was once astonished to hear a quite well-known breeder describe a twelve-week-old HPR puppy that had received no training whatever to a prospective buyer as having been 'shot over'. In most shooting men's minds a bird dog which has been 'shot over' means one that has been trained to the stage where it has actually found, pointed and produced live game for a gun to shoot. The breeder's definition was that the puppy had, at some time in its short life, heard the sound of a gunshot. There was no intention to mislead the buyer, simply a misunderstanding of the term 'shot over'.

So take good care that you and the seller are both on the same wavelength. What, for example, does it mean if the trainer says that the dog is trained to retrieve, or is retrieving? It could mean that the dog has experience of picking up on a shoot, or it could mean that it has not yet progressed beyond retrieving a dummy. Similarly, 'quite steady' might mean steady to the toss of a dummy, it might mean steady to flush or to shot, or it might mean that the dog will sit happily by your side while dead pheasants rain down all around it. It is up to you to be certain that what you are hearing is what the seller is saying.

A dog may be offered for sale at any stage in its training. At the most basic level it might have had no more done with it than being taught to sit, to stay, to come when called and to walk to heel. Note particularly that house training may not feature in the training schedule of even the most experienced shooting dog. In many professional and amateur training establishments the dogs will live all their lives in kennels. If you are planning to keep your dog in your house you should check whether it has been house trained; if not be prepared for a few days or weeks of vigilance before you can feel that your carpets are safe.

The next stage up from the basics is the dog which has been taken through the obedience disciplines of gundog work but which has not yet been introduced to the field. There are no hard and fast rules to govern what aspects of work such a dog will have covered, and it is up to the buyer and the seller to clarify this. Take our earlier example of the dog that has been taught to retrieve. Does this mean that it will perform the basic obedience test type retrieve, i.e. stay steady while a dummy is thrown, go and collect it on command and bring it straight back to the handler? Or does it mean that it can mark and remember half a dozen dummies, collect them in the order specified by its trainer, hunt out cover for an unseen retrieve, be handled onto a distant mark by voice, whistle or hand signal and collect a dummy from in or across water?

There is also a wide variety of interpretation of the concept of an introduction to shooting, and of the idea of the dog that has been trained but not yet entered to the shooting field. Does 'trained but not entered' in this instance imply that the dog will have been introduced to the sound of gunfire, that it will have been worked on cold game or that it will have learned to hunt free and drop to flush? It may do, but a dog that has done none of those things could still quite fairly be described as trained but not yet entered.

And what about the dog that has been introduced to shooting? Does that mean it has spent a day or two standing well behind the line at a small driven shoot and perhaps collected one or two easy retrieves? Does it mean that it has gradually been brought on until it is ready for a proper day's work picking up or even hunting in the beating line? Or does it mean that it was taken out and figuratively thrown in at the deep end just so that when it is sold it can be described as an 'experienced shooting dog'?

In case I seem to be suggesting that the world is filled with unscrupulous gundog trainers waiting to pounce on unsuspecting buyers and palm them off with a half-trained field trial reject, let me emphasise that this is not my intention. The great majority of trainers will not advertise a dog as trained or ready for work unless it is worthy of the description. Apart from any legal considerations, or the damage that selling a badly trained dog might do to their reputations, any sensible buyer is going to insist on seeing a demonstration of the dog's abilities before parting with his money.

There are two stages that every prospective buyer of a trained dog should follow. The first is to ensure that you understand quite clearly what the seller means when he says the dog is trained. What will the dog do, what practical experience has it had, and, if applicable, what further work does the seller feel it requires? Both parties must be quite clear as to exactly what is on offer.

The second stage is for the trainer to take the dog out and let the buyer see it at work. The demonstration serves two purposes. First, it allows the seller to show the buyer that the dog really will do the things he has claimed. Secondly, and equally importantly, it allows the trainer to teach the new owner how to handle the dog: what make of whistle to use and how to employ it; what hand signals and voice commands the dog understands; how much handling the dog requires. Dogs, however well trained, are individuals and must be treated as such.

You should make sure that the demonstration is detailed enough to give a real indication of the dog's abilities. Walking a few yards at heel across the lawn and collecting a couple of dummies in a grass field is not enough, particularly if the dog is supposed to be fully trained and experienced. Indeed, if you are buying a dog which is claimed to be experienced in the shooting field it is not unreasonable to ask for the demonstration to be made in the most appropriate place – on a proper shooting day. This may not be possible – you may be buying the dog during the close season – but if you can arrange to see the dog actually at work then do so. If you are buying it outside the shooting season – and this is not a bad option since it will allow you to build up a rapport with it before you start working it – it is well worth trying to arrange for the trainer to come along and show you how to work the dog once shooting starts again.

Having Your Pup Professionally Trained

An alternative to either training your own dog or buying one ready-trained is to purchase a puppy and then send it to a profes-

Shared shooting experience should build a keen rapport between owner and dog.

sional trainer when it is ready to begin its education.

This is an option that will appeal particularly to those owners who enjoy the challenge and rewards of raising a puppy but who lack the time, facilities or ability to train it on to the standard of gundog work that they require. It is somewhat more risky than buying a fully trained dog since, by the time the pup is ready to send off to boarding school it is likely to have become such a member of the family that you are stuck with it for the next ten to fifteen years regardless of how well it finally does. And of course, you have to raise the pup from eight weeks through to nine months or a year old before it is ready to start its training.

Apart from any accidents or illnesses that might strike during that interim period there is also the danger that you may make the professional trainer's task harder because of the way you have raised the pup. If it is used to running wild and ignoring commands at home the trainer will have to overcome those problems before he can start to make any progress. This may not be such a problem as it might appear, since the pup will be going into a new environment, with a new and experienced trainer in charge. Although it may think it is the leader of the pack in its own home it will not be allowed to assume that mantle in the training kennels.

Much further down the line, when it has finished its education and has come home to live, it may well decide that it can reassert its former authority over its human 'pack'. This is a hurdle that will have to be overcome should it arise, but the fact that the dog has accepted the authority of the trainer ought to make it easier for the owner to take control himself. It would of course be far better if the pup had never been allowed to assume a dominant role in the family right from the beginning.

Most trainers will want to spend a few weeks with the dog, getting to know it and assessing its potential before committing themselves to training it. It is important that trainer and owner agree in advance on what end result is required. Are you planning to enter it in field trials or working tests, or do you just want a dog that will sit beside you at driven pheasant shoots and retrieve the odd bird? Do you want to be able to handle it out into the far distance, or is all your shooting done at the kind of establishment that employs a team of pickers up for anything that is not lying close to the pegs? There is no point in spending a lot of money having the dog trained in every aspect of retriever work if all you want it to do is sit with you in a pigeon hide, though there is no reason why such a dog should not be fully trained if you wish and can afford it.

The other side of this particular equation concerns the limitations of the dog. It is one thing to instruct a professional trainer to take your pup and turn it into a field trial champion, but it is quite another for the trainer to succeed. Those first three or four weeks will allow the trainer to make a rough assessment of what he can make of your pup, but only as the training progresses can he really begin to see what limitations there are to its progress. A good trainer will keep you informed, particularly if it feels that the finished dog may not match your expectations.

No matter whether you buy a trained dog or have a puppy trained specially, the time will come eventually when the dog is passed into your care. Months of work and probably much money have gone into bringing it to the stage where it passes out from training camp and is ready to take shooting. Except that taking it shooting is not a good idea just at the moment.

Before you take it out on the shoot you have to establish some sort of rapport with it. It has been used to working for its trainer; listening for his voice and his particular whistle and watching his hand signals. Now you are taking over and no matter how carefully you try to copy the commands and gestures taught you by

A well-trained pair of Labradors enjoying an autumn morning walk around the shoot.

the trainer the dog will know that you are not 'the boss'. Not yet. You have to work together for a while, retrieving a few dummies, doing some sits and stays and some heel work, checking that it recognises and obeys your drop whistle. Do this well away from the distractions of live game, other dogs being handled, guns going off and birds falling out of the sky. The dog's attention needs to be firmly on you (and yours on it) until you have established that 'the boss' is now you. *Then* you can think about taking it shooting.

149

The same restrictions apply to introducing a professionally trained dog to the shooting field as to one that you have trained yourself. Even if you have bought a dog with a couple of season's work behind it you should never assume that it will settle down effortlessly to working for you. Leave your gun at home the first time you take it out, just as if you were starting off with a raw novice, and give all your attention to the dog. You may lose a day's shooting, but it is well worth it if it allows you to establish a proper working relationship with your new dog. The shooting will be a matter of history by the end of the afternoon; your partnership with the dog will hopefully endure for the next ten years or more.

8

Field Days

Whatever sport you may pursue,
There'll be a gundog just for you,
To sit beside your peg, or rush,
Around in frantic haste, and flush,
Or maybe point, your grouse and pheasant,
And make your shooting far more pleasant.

David Hudson

Some people, such as professional gundog trainers, game-keepers, deerstalkers, shepherds and the like, keep dogs because their chosen profession requires it. In most cases they will at the very least have had an interest in dogs and dog work before electing to follow one of these demanding and generally poorly paid callings, though to some a working dog is simply a tool of their trade – something to be fetched from the kennel when needed and pretty much ignored for the rest of the time.

For a shepherd's collies 'when needed' could mean every day of the year, whereas a keeper's terriers might only be required for a few days in the spring when clearing out fox dens. Where they spend the rest of the year will depend on the whim of their owner, and might of course mean that they live in the house like any family pet. But whether they work a gentleman's hours or have to flog away day after day like slaves, these dogs are bred, trained and worked because they are necessary in order for a job to be done.

In contrast to the professionals, for the vast majority of gundog owners their dogs are something of an indulgence. We keep our dogs through choice, not necessity, and we keep them because of the pleasure they give us. Or perhaps I should say because of the pleasure we hope they will give us, since the reality may not always live up to the dream.

I will be the first to admit that there are times when pleasure is not the emotion that is uppermost in my mind when working my gundogs. When you are stumbling across a 40 acre ploughed field with 10 lb of mud on each boot and an icy rain trickling down your neck, trying to catch a recalcitrant puppy which is dancing around you and keeping carefully just out of your reach I rather doubt that you will be musing on the pleasures of owning a Labrador. When it leaps onto the back seat of your new car after rolling luxuriously in a long-dead sheep carcass I suspect that even you may have doubts about the delights of keeping a dog.

The same feelings may arise when it takes off in hot pursuit of a hare just as the keeper has asked everyone to 'keep their dogs in please', or starts running in to the fall of game despite all the months you have spent trying to make it steady. Keeping a working gundog can sometimes put a heavy load on your patience and good humour.

There is a distinction between the two types of problem outlined above. When the puppy runs away and challenges you to catch it it is simply indulging a natural inclination to play with the other members of its pack. When it rolls in the dead sheep it is responding to instincts handed down through the centuries from the wolves that were its ancestors. In effect it is behaving naturally and probably thinks that you will be pleased to be included in the game, or to share the aroma of rotten mutton with it. In contrast, when it chases the hare or runs in to the shot pheasant, although it is still obeying its instincts, it is doing so in the full knowledge that it should not be behaving in that manner. (I am assuming here that you have done at least some training prior to taking the dog shooting). While both types of problem are annoying I am personally more upset by the deliberate flaunting of authority, not least because I know that I am at least as much to blame as the dog.

But hopefully the minutes of hair-tearing frustration will be greatly outnumbered by the hours of pleasure both at home and out on the shoot. The owner who keeps his dog in a kennel and only takes it out on shooting days is missing out on a great deal of the fun of keeping a Labrador. After all, there are 365 days in a year. Even if you are fortunate enough to shoot twice a week from August to January that will only account for forty or fifty days, say 11 or 12 per cent of the year. That leaves almost 90 per cent of the year when you will not be enjoying your dog's company if it is spending all its time shut away in the kennel.

A Labrador is particularly well suited to serve as both family dog and worker. Pointers and setters are great characters but they are much harder work than a Labrador. Exercise to a pointer or setter means running, and the more running the better. The next field is always much more interesting than the one it is in, and the one after that looks positively inviting. They need to be watched all the time when they are out walking, and reined in before they disappear into the next parish, or possibly the next county. In contrast, Bess, my current Labrador, will potter along happily for hours, more or less at heel, with the absolute minimum of fuss or supervision.

A sunny afternoon in the garden will see Bess picking a comfortable spot on the lawn, stretching out and dozing off in the sunshine. She may look as if she is fast asleep, but she is always aware of where I am and what I am doing. She keeps an eye on me, and if I go out of the garden for some reason she will be there with me. Take Ghillie, one of the pointer bitches, out into the garden and I have to spend all afternoon with one eye on her in case she gets bored with harassing the local songbirds and decides to go and explore Scotland.

Doctors are now 'discovering' what dog owners have known for years: that keeping a dog is good for your health. The exercise, the company and the calming influence all contribute to lowering your blood pressure and steadying your heartbeat. A dog in the house will improve your physical and mental health, and of all the gundog breeds a Labrador is arguably the best suited to the dual role of family dog and worker.

I know that a lot of people will disagree with that last statement, but I did say 'arguably' the best suited. One can make a case for one of the spaniel breeds, for the Golden or the Flatcoated Retriever, one of the HPRs or even a pointer or setter for those with masochistic tendencies. I am sure there are proud owners of Pit Bull Terriers who would swear on a stack of bibles that there was no better dog for a children's pet or an old lady's companion. Even so, if you want a gundog that will double as a family pet you are unlikely to go wrong with a Labrador. And remember that your Labrador is probably going to be cast in that family pet role for over ninety per cent of the time, even if you are buying it primarily as a shooting dog.

But it is out in the shooting field that you will forge the partnership that will bind you together. Years after the rest of the day has been forgotten, when you can no longer remember who you were shooting with, what the bag totalled, perhaps not even where it all took place, you will still remember with complete clarity a particular piece of work: the look on the dog's face as it finally picked the winged grouse that had been twisting and turning through the peat hags, or swam back across the swollen river with the mallard drake in its mouth. Something will stir your memories

Waiting patiently and marking carefully until ordered to retrieve.

of a long gone old friend and a picture will surface in your mind. 'Old Charlie? I'll never forget the day when he . . .'

And of course it may not always be the triumphs that you remember best. I was once shooting on a keeper's day at the very end of the season. We were taking a long wood through, away from the release pen towards a line of guns waiting beyond a distant line of beech trees. I was left at a corner of the wood as a back gun in case any birds broke over the beating line and headed for their old haunts around the pen. It was a sunny winter afternoon, there were red squirrels playing in the branches, and I was not paying as much attention as I should have been, so when a cock pheasant suddenly glided round the corner on set wings I was slow to raise the gun.

He flared up and was about to drop down and land in the wood as I fired. I had no idea whether I had hit him or not because he disappeared into the trees just as I pulled the trigger. There was a dry-stone wall between the wood and where I was standing so I could see nothing at all at ground level. I had to stay out in the field, ready for anything else that flew back, until the beaters had finished the wood so I decided to send Bess in to retrieve it – if indeed it was there to be retrieved. I sent her on over the wall, told her 'hi lost' and waited. A couple of minutes later she returned, empty-mouthed. Not convinced that she had conducted a proper search I sent her back in again. There was a longer interval and a certain amount of crashing about in the undergrowth and then the black face popped over the wall again. Still no pheasant. I sent her back for one last try. There was more snuffling about, getting fainter as she searched a wider area. Then triumph. She bounded back over the wall and delivered . . . a dead rabbit.

It had been dead for quite some time, but naturally I had to take it from her and tell her what a good dog she had been. And so she had. As for the pheasant, I am sure now that I should have realised what Bess knew all along: that I had missed him cleanly and he had taken off running as soon as he landed. But in her mind I apparently wanted her to retrieve something and she was determined not to let me down.

One of the most memorable pieces of work I have ever seen a Labrador perform happened on 12 August on a grouse moor in Perthshire. The grouse were not exactly abundant that year and the pointers had been working exceptionally hard in still, humid conditions, with little scent to help them find birds. There were a few late broods that were too young to be shot just to make things even more complicated, but by mid-afternoon a bit of a breeze had risen and the bag was beginning to mount up. We were working downwind on our way back to where the cars were parked when a single bird rose from the face of a little hillock we were about to descend.

One of the guns fired and hit the grouse, which shed a cloud of feathers but struggled on for a couple of hundred yards before pitching down on a heathery bank the other side of a narrow valley. A local handler who trains his dogs for trials as well as for ordinary work had come along to pick up that day and we all stopped to watch as he handled his bitch out to the fall. She was only a youngster, but she was beautifully trained and obeyed every whistle and every hand signal as if she were connected to her owner by some form of remote control. He sent her out until she was roughly in the area where we had marked the grouse to ground, then pipped on his whistle to tell her to sit. Then he moved her a few yards this way and a few yards that until she was right on the spot, whereupon she picked the bird and raced back to him to deliver it.

We then cast one of the pointers off, ready to start out again and she pointed immediately, no more than 10 yards (9 m) from where we had all been standing, admiring the handleability of the little Labrador bitch. We assumed that she was pointing the spot where the dead grouse had been sitting before it was flushed, but remembering the maxim 'always trust your dog' we sent two guns forward to check things out. The pointer moved a couple of steps and a covey of ten grouse burst out of the heather almost under her feet. Not only had they sat there while we all stood and watched the retrieve, but the Labrador had run right through them twice – once on the way out and again on the way back.

It told us something about the relative 'noses' of Labradors and pointers, though to be fair the Labrador handler had already said that his bitch did not have the best of noses – hence the need to handle her right onto the fall rather than push her out a few yards downwind of it and leave her to work it out for herself – but even so it was an impressive piece of work and one that has stuck in my mind ever since.

It was impressive at least in part because, being out on the open hill, we were able to stand and watch every move: not something that is generally possible on a low-ground shoot. By its very nature some of the best Labrador work will be unseen. When a pheasant is dropped with a broken wing and runs into thick cover we have no way of knowing what happens when we send our dog in to collect it. It may be lying dead 10 yards (9 m) into the wood, or it may have run for ½ mile (1 km). It may be the only pheasant in there, or the dog may have to pick out the one wounded bird from among dozens of healthy ones. All we see is the dog clearing the fence one way, then coming back a few seconds or perhaps a few minutes later with the wounded bird in its mouth. Who knows what wonders have been performed in the interval?

All too often, though, the most abiding memory of the dogs on a shooting day may have nothing to do with top-quality training or brilliant individual performances. The most memorable dog may make a lasting impression for all the wrong reasons.

Imagine a driven pheasant shoot. The guns are lined up along the foot of a little valley below a wood. The sound of voices and the tapping of sticks tells us that the beaters have begun their advance through the trees and after a few moments the sound of urgent wings and a shout of 'over' tells us that the first pheasant is on its way. It rises high over the trees and starts to glide across the valley with the shelter of a distant wood as its destination. One of the guns swings onto it; there is the sharp crack of a shot and the pheasant throws its head back and thumps down onto the grass 40 yards behind the gun who shot it. What will happen next?

Ideally nothing at all until the beaters flush the next bird. The pheasant is dead, in plain sight, and can be collected at the end of the drive. If the gun who shot it has a retriever with him he may elect to send the dog to collect the bird, though he would probably be better to keep his full attention on his shooting. If there is a picker up back behind the line he should be watching for runners or pricked birds that may need to be collected quickly and not bothering about obviously dead birds at this stage in the drive. Our pheasant should really lie there until the keeper's whistle signals the end of the drive, and then be collected by the dog belonging to the gun who killed it. But will it? Let us consider another couple of scenarios that may not be unfamiliar to you.

Perhaps the retriever sitting with the gun who killed the pheasant will run in unbidden and collect it as soon as it realises that the bird has been killed. Worse: perhaps one of the other guns' dogs will race across and poach it. Worse still, but not unknown: one of the beaters' dogs may come bursting out of the wood and grab the dead pheasant. And finally, all of this may happen, more or less simultaneously, possibly combined with a dog fight, a great deal of shouting from all quarters and quite likely a dismembered pheasant as a result.

These little incidents can cause a certain amount of tension, depending on the sort of shoot and the attitude of the guns to their dogs. On an informal knock-about day where the guns are all friends and the bag is unlikely to be more than a few birds, everyone

If your dog starts running in it is a simple matter to prevent it.

may be fairly relaxed about such events. Wild dogs and stolen retrieves may be no more than something to laugh about over lunch. On a commercial shoot, with guns paying a great deal of money to shoot a bag of several hundred birds, a dog running wild may disrupt the entire day.

Different people have different ideas about what is acceptable behaviour from their dogs on a shooting day. If you are a stickler for discipline and insist that your dog stays at your side until you send it to collect a shot bird you are unlikely to be impressed when the dog from three guns along the line races up and steals your birds. If your dog, which is similarly unimpressed, decides that it had better get there first if it is to have any chance of a retrieve and starts running in, it is entirely possible that tempers may rise and words be exchanged between the parties involved. Some guns get very upset if their dog is not given at least first chance to collect the game they shoot.

Some dogs lack discipline. Whether this is because they have not been properly trained or because their owners cannot or will not make the effort to control them is not important: the end result is the same. A lack of discipline can vary from a dog that is normally quite steady but will sneak off for a retrieve if it thinks the owner is not paying attention to one that runs totally wild. Who has not seen some wild brute charging about behind the guns with 3 ft of rope and a corkscrew dog tether flailing about behind it? At least in this case the rope and the tether suggest that the owner has made an effort to keep his dog under control. Some owners seem to be completely oblivious to the wishes of their fellow guns and leave their dogs loose throughout the drive, wandering where they will and picking up and sometimes discarding game as it takes their fancy.

Apart from the torn hair and raised blood pressure that this can induce among the other guns, this type of behaviour makes life very difficult when picking up at the end of the drive. It can be hard enough to pick every bird, even when you know roughly where they should be. If no one is sure which birds have been retrieved and which may have been picked up and dropped somewhere else a proper gathering becomes almost impossible. To make matters even more complicated, some dogs will refuse to collect game that has already been mouthed by another.

Bad discipline is infectious among gundogs. Imagine the feelings going through your dog's mind when it is sitting by your peg. It watches a pheasant gliding overhead; sees you put up the gun and bring it thumping down to the ground behind it. That bird is now registered in its brain as the property of *its* pack – the 'pack' in this case consisting of you and it. Being properly trained it remains sitting beside you, but by now it is quivering with excitement and the anticipation of the retrieve. And then another dog races up and makes off with 'its' bird. What is it going to be tempted to do next time you fire a shot? You will obviously be concentrating on the pheasant, so the chances are you will not realise that your dog has broken ranks until it is well on its way. If you are quick enough you may be able to stop it and call it back, but if it reaches the shot bird and collects it you have a problem. It is going to retrieve it now and if you tell it off it is going to assume that it is in trouble for retrieving: not for running in. But if you do not let it know that it is wrong to run in it may decide that it has neatly solved the problem of other dogs stealing its birds and start running in for everything.

Bess, my current Labrador, is inclined to run in, so I normally loop a lead over her neck and tie it to my stick when I am standing at a drive. It is more of a token than a need actually to tie her down so that she cannot run in. Provided that she thinks she is under control she will sit reasonably well and not try to rip the stick out of the ground when a bird falls. On some drives I leave her loose if I know there will be no harm done if she takes off after any bird I happen to kill. Fortunately she is not inclined to poach from other guns: only my birds are considered her personal property to be collected at the first opportunity.

We were shooting one very cold, wet day and on the final drive I decided to leave her free because the birds would be curving back over my peg and into a very dense wood and any runner might need to be picked pretty smartly. Bess can be pretty smart, given the right incentive. As it happened I was drawn next to a dog that treated every retrieve as his own, so Bess had not seen much action during the rest of the day. A hen pheasant curled back over me and I shot it. Bess, as expected, trotted off to collect, only to be shoulder charged off it at the last moment by my neighbour's dog. She watched him race off with it with that peculiarly sad expression that only a cold, wet and now disappointed Labrador can assume, and then, instead of coming back to sit by my peg, she very point-edly took up a position 30 yards ahead of me. 'Next time,' she seemed to be saying, 'I am going to have a head start on him.' Sadly, there was no next time as that was the only bird that came my way on what was the final drive of the day, but her reasoning was sound.

The whole purpose for a shooting day is enjoyment. The guns, beaters and pickers up will all be there because they want to be part of the day: to shoot, to work their dogs or just to enjoy the company and perhaps put a few pounds into their pockets or a brace of birds into the larder at the end of the day. For the keepers and the shoot manager things are slightly different as a shoot day is the culmination of a lot of hard work, but provided things run according to plan, a shoot day should be a pleasure for the profes-sionals involved as well as the amateurs.

There can be few gundog owners whose enjoyment of a day's shooting is not greatly enhanced when their dogs work well. If you have trained your own dog you will have invested a great deal of time in its education; if you bought a trained dog your invest-ment will be in money rather than time. In either case, though, you will have a strong interest in seeing the best results from that investment. When your dog is working well you are free to concentrate on your shooting, and will almost certainly shoot better as a result. And what dog owner does not like to hear someone praising his dog? If someone says 'That was a smart piece of work' or 'Hasn't your dog worked well?' it rounds off the day

A job well done for this picker up and his Labrador on a gloomy, December afternoon.

with a pleasant glow. Contrast that with your feelings when you have spent the day apologising to your neighbours because your dog has poached their game or being berated by the keeper because your dog charged off through the wood and ruined the best drive of the day.

You may shoot in circumstances where there are no other guns and no keepers to approve or disapprove of your dog's behaviour. For the wildfowler out on the foreshore or the pigeon shooter sitting under a hedge with his decoys spread out in front of him the only judge of their dogs will be themselves. Even so, the dog that sits quietly at their side until bidden will give far more satisfaction than one that must be tied down to stop it racing off every time the gun is fired, or one that whines constantly and fidgets instead of settling down patiently. And when you are sitting alone in the darkness of the estuary with no sound but the wind, the waves and the haunting cries of the seabirds, a warm nose pressed into your hand and the solid presence of a Labrador by your side is a great comfort.

If you enjoy working your dog with just each other for company you should enquire whether the shoot you are involved with needs

Reliable dogs and reliable handlers are in demand at almost every shoot.

any help to pick up on the day following the shoot. Wounded birds that flew on and were not picked at the time may have died overnight, or have recovered enough to be out and about again the next morning. Volunteers to make a sweep through the coverts the day after the shoot are often welcome. Such work can be excellent experience for your dog provided that it is not allowed to cause havoc among the healthy birds that are creeping back into their normal haunts. If you are going back the next day make sure that you check with the keeper first to see if there are any no-go areas that you must avoid.

There is a place for the properly trained, well-behaved Labrador on practically every shoot in the country. From the smallest of rough shoots where a couple of guns walk the hedgerows for an odd rabbit or the chance of a stray pheasant, to the grand commercial enterprise where eight guns are paying in excess of twenty thousand pounds for a day's shooting, there will be a niche for the working Labrador.

Reliable dogs – and reliable handlers – are in demand at practically every shoot. If you have a good, steady dog that will not run riot in the coverts or poach retrieves from the paying guns, then you can probably find work for it on as many days as you can get away from your work or your other responsibilities, right through the shooting season. In contrast, if you cannot, or will not, control your dog then you may find that the only shoots that will welcome you will be those where no one else controls their dogs either. And while the dogs may have a great time on such shoots they are generally not much fun for the guns and the handlers.

Training a Labrador takes time, patience and a certain amount of physical effort, but it could never be fairly described as hard work. Anyone who can spare fifteen minutes each day – about one per cent of the twenty-four hours available – has ample time to train a gundog. And if you are so busy that it is impossible to find fifteen minutes a day then perhaps you should not be keeping a dog at all. Even if you have the kind of job that means you have to work away from home during the week and only have time for dog training at the weekends it is still quite possible for you to turn your puppy into a top-quality gundog, though you may have to spend a bit more than fifteen minutes with it on the days that you do have available.

Throughout this book I have been stressing the need to proceed slowly through training: to introduce the dog gradually to the shooting field and to try at all times to keep it properly under control. All this takes patience, especially when you are itching to see your protégé getting down to some real work. It is certainly a lot easier for the owner/trainer who takes a more laissez-faire attitude and does not worry too much if his dog runs a little wild or has to be kept tethered throughout every drive. Is there really any need for the gun who is not interested in field trials or in the finer points of dog work to try that hard to keep his dog properly in hand?

Let us consider the advantages of a well-trained, properly behaved Labrador. If you have full confidence in your dog's steadiness you will be able to give your total attention to your shooting instead of having to keep one eye on the dog. So just to start with, your shooting should improve. It does not matter whether you are standing at a peg firing cartridges by the hundred or walking up on a rough-shooting day and only getting a shot here and there; if you know that your dog will sit staunchly throughout the drive, or drop smartly to every flushed bird, then you will shoot with far greater freedom – and hopefully with a correspondingly greater measure of success.

Satisfaction all round at the sight of a well-filled game cart.

Then there is the matter of the birds you shoot. The wild dog may be an excellent natural retriever, deadly on every runner and practically guaranteed to pick every bird shot. The well-trained dog may have a poor nose and lack the drive necessary to hunt down a strong running pheasant. Some dogs do have more natural ability than others, just as some men shoot better than their companions. However, a wild dog would be far better if it were properly trained and controlled. And a lack of natural ability can, in some ways, be at least partly overcome if the dog can be easily handled out to the fall of game.

A dog that sits throughout the drive and marks every bird you shoot will pick more efficiently than one that tears off after the first pheasant over and does not see the next two or three to fall. When a winged pheasant is running for a distant covert there is a considerable advantage for the owner who can set his dog straight off to collect that particular bird and not have it waste time collecting two or three that are lying dead in plain sight around the peg first. So a well-trained dog should pick a higher percentage of the game you kill than its wild brother – assuming that they have similar natural ability. A well-trained dog will put more game into your game bag.

There are indirect benefits as well. There is a spare place for a good dog on almost every shoot. Once you establish a foothold on one shoot, provided that you and your dog do a good job in a proper, controlled manner, there is every chance of your being invited to other shoots in the area. Imagine that a neighbouring keeper is short of beaters or pickers up and phones the keeper from 'your' shoot to ask if he knows anyone who can help out. Who is he more likely to recommend: the owner of a well-trained dog or the owner of one that ruined two drives by running wild or caused one of the guns to blow his top by 'stealing' all his birds before his own dog could retrieve them?

Invitations to shoot can also be won or lost on the manners of your dog. Whether it is the owner of a shoot drawing up a list of guns to invite for a weekend shooting party or a member of a syndicate wondering who to ask along on their guest day, the likely performance of the dog may have as much influence on their choice as the ability of the gun. 'The trouble is; if we ask Joe, he'll bring that blasted dog along with him. Remember last time when it . . .' And so Joe loses out to someone else whose dog can be trusted; and of course, he will never know for sure why he has not been invited again. So a wild dog can severely curtail your shooting invitations while a well-mannered one may positively increase them.

But all that may be of little interest to you. Perhaps you have as much shooting as you want, with a team of pickers up on every shoot to worry about collecting every last bird that is hit. Perhaps you do all your shooting on your own, on a rough shoot, in a pigeon hide or out on the foreshore. Perhaps you are one of those people who simply could not give a damn what anyone else thinks of them, their dog, or the way the dog has been performing. Even so, there is still one definite inducement to owning and working a properly trained and behaved dog: there is the matter of your own, personal satisfaction.

Everyone can take pleasure from a job well done. It may not make any practical difference if your dog charges off in pursuit of a pheasant the instant you raise your gun, or if it sits, alert and eager, but under control until you click your fingers and tell it to get on. But it looks better and it feels much more satisfying even if there is no one around to see it except yourself. When the dog

Waiting for the off and hoping that the day will work out well.

gets it absolutely right in front of the gallery, especially if it gets it right where others have been consistently getting it wrong, there is an even greater frisson of satisfaction. And when someone says, offhand or casual as it may be, 'Your dog is working well today', or 'That was a smart piece of work', then I defy any owner in the land not to be at least a little bit elevated by the compliment.

Practically everyone involved in a shooting day is present because shooting is their hobby – and often a hobby that costs them a considerable sum to follow. Even those such as beaters or pickers up who are paid to take part will not be along solely for the money. But whether paying or being paid, everyone will be there with the principal aim of enjoying themselves. No matter how casual their attitude, practically every owner of a working gundog will be hoping that their dog – or dogs – will do their job, do it well, and do it in style.

It takes considerable expenditure of time and not a little effort to bring a puppy on from raw novice to accomplished gundog, but that effort will be more than repaid when, finally, you can go shooting with every confidence that you and your dog, in partnership, can get the job done, and get it done to everybody's satisfaction.

Not least your own.

9

And Finally . . .

He isn't hard-mouthed: he just takes a firm hold,
And he's really not vicious: just stubborn, and bold,
He doesn't run in: he's just quick off the mark,
And he never would point at a pipit, or lark,
They just happened to be there, right under his nose,
When he pointed a grouse, or a blackcock, which rose,
Well ahead, where it couldn't be seen,
And he'd not missed those birds, he just hadn't been,
Over that bit of ground: he'd have come back and done it,
Except for the hare, and he'd never have run it,
So far, if he hadn't have known, from the scent,
That it must have been wounded: yes, I know that it went,
Like a bat out of hell, but that isn't to say,
That it hadn't been shot on some previous day.
He's not out of control, he's just getting well out,
He'd turn to the whistle, or maybe a shout,
If I gave one, but really I don't want to drop him,
This is quality work, and I'd rather not stop him,
And I'm sure he'll come back into sight before long.
Well, you know: I'm the first to admit, when he's wrong.

David Hudson

One or two people – invariably those who have seen my own Labrador at work – have wondered, gently, why I am writing a book about Labradors. The simple answer to the question is that I was asked to do so, but the real reason lies deeper.

Every week, from August through to the end of January, thousands of amateur handlers are out working their dogs on shoots throughout the length and breadth of Britain. Among them will be dogs trained to the sort of standard that wins field trials, and dogs that are so wild that the other members of the shoot dread them making an appearance. These are the opposite ends of the spectrum, and in between are the great majority of working gundogs: not perfect, not by any means useless, but simply doing their job to the best of their own and their owners' abilities.

They may not be destined to win field trial awards, but that is not their owners' aim in any case. They just enjoy working their dogs.

As a member of that majority I am well aware of my own dog's failings: a certain lack of steadiness, a tendency to skirt round the thickest cover unless she is sure there is a pheasant in residence, and intermittent, selective deafness, especially when there are birds running ahead of her in a covert. I would much prefer that she did not work to her own agenda whenever the mood overtakes her, and on occasion I know that the long-suffering Douglas MacMillan, who keepers the best pheasant shoot in the south of Scotland, would agree with me. He is, of course, far too polite to say so.

However, the fact that my own dog falls short of my own ideals should not disqualify me from writing about the theory and principles of training. In this I am reminded of an acquaintance from many years ago who was an acknowledged expert on racing form. Before a race he could tell you exactly which horse would win – and after the race he could tell you exactly why it did not. I knew exactly what I wanted from Bess when I trained her, and now I have a very good idea of where I went wrong. I suspect, though, that I will make exactly the same mistakes again whenever the time comes to start again. And if not the same mistakes I am sure I will find some new ones.

Over the years I have read an awful lot of books and articles concerned with dog training, mostly written by *real* experts, who have strings of field trial champions to their names, and that uncanny ability, gifted to only a few, of getting the very best out of any dog placed in their care. In general, they tend to preach a counsel of perfection, assuming that every amateur dog trainer is aiming at the same high standards that they achieve themselves. Now, while we amateurs may be aiming high, the majority of us know in our hearts that our actual achievements are going to fall some way short of our original aim. Nevertheless, we do not let that stop us from trying.

The great majority of amateur trainers will never reach the standards of the professional handlers simply because they lack the time, the talent, the experience and the facilities to do so. In many cases they are more interested in shooting than in dog training, and are quite happy to settle for a dog that, though it might not last ten seconds in a field trial, works perfectly well as far as they are concerned. If your dog does what *you* want it to do, then it matters not a whit if it can never win a field trial, a working test, or indeed a show bench award. If you are happy with your dog then it is a good dog, and to hell with what anyone else thinks.

Even better, if the other dog owners at the shoot also think it's a good dog, then you have pretty much got it made.

So that is the point of this book: to prompt you to decide what you want from your dog and, hopefully, to help you attain it. And if, like Bess and me, the reality is not quite up to the level of the dream, then just get on and enjoy the good times while not worrying unduly about the others. At least I know she is enjoying herself.

Index